POLICY AND PRACTICE IN HEALTH AND SOCIAL CARE
NUMBER THIRTEEN

Supporting Vulnerable Adults:
Citizenship, Capacity, Choice

POLICY AND PRACTICE IN HEALTH AND SOCIAL CARE

POLICY AND PRACTICE IN HEALTH AND SOCIAL CARE

SERIES EDITORS

JOYCE CAVAYE and ALISON PETCH

Supporting Vulnerable Adults: Citizenship, Capacity, Choice

Ailsa Stewart

Glasgow School of Social Work,
University of Strathclyde

DUNEDIN

Published by
Dunedin Academic Press Ltd
Hudson House
8 Albany Street
Edinburgh EH1 3QB
Scotland

ISBN: 978–1–906716–12–7
ISSN 1750–1407

First published 2012
British Library Cataloguing in Publication data
A catalogue record for this book is available from the British Library

Typeset by Makar Publishing Production
Printed in Great Britain by CPI Antony Rowe

CONTENTS

SERIES EDITORS' INTRODUCTION

Scotland has been at the forefront of legislation concerned to provide support and protection for those who may be at risk of harm. The first major piece of legislation from the new Scottish Parliament was the Adults with Incapacity (Scotland) Act 2000, while the Adult Support and Protection (Scotland) Act 2007 has provided a legislative base for Scotland while others still debate the necessity of such a measure. This volume takes as its central point this latter Act and explores core issues such as capacity and choice in the context of different understandings of citizenship. It offers a detailed scrutiny, which can be read in tandem with the more general overview of civil mental health and incapacity legislation offered by Atkinson (2006) in an earlier volume in this series.

The discussion draws on original research conducted by the author that provides a depth and resonance to the argument. It also draws on a number of case studies and a number of enquiries into individual situations to locate the discussion in the realities of practice.

Following an introductory historical overview, Ailsa Stewart addresses the definitional debates in this area and associated sensitivities. She then explores key elements of the various adult protections systems across the UK and discusses the role of legislation. This analysis highlights the increasing divergence between Scotland and the rest of the UK but also identifies a common concern in respect of the appropriate balance between autonomy and protection. The interplay across the key themes of risk, vulnerability, capacity and citizenship in the emergence of the Adult Support and Protection (Scotland) Act 2007 is tracked, and the volume concludes with a discussion of a range of tensions and challenges to be observed and addressed as implementation of the legislation proceeds.

Dr Joyce Cavaye
Faculty of Health and Social Care, The Open University in Scotland, Edinburgh

Professor Alison Petch
The Institute for Research and Innovation in Social Services (IRISS), Glasgow

ACKNOWLEDGEMENTS

My sincere gratitude goes to the busy professionals who gave of their time to be interviewed and to complete the on-line survey for the main research for this book, with particular thanks to Jean McClellan and her colleagues at the Scottish Government for their support. Grateful appreciation also to Professor Jacqueline Atkinson and Alison Petch for their advice and encouragement. Finally, my grateful thanks to my husband Sandy for his patience and understanding over many evenings and weekends.

GLOSSARY OF ABBREVIATIONS

ADASS	Association of Directors of Adult Social Services
ADSS	Association of Directors of Social Services
AEA	Action on Elder Abuse
APC	Adult Protection Committee
ASP	Adult Support and Protection (Scotland) Act 2007
AWIA	Adults with Incapacity (Scotland) Act 2000
BME	Black and Minority Ethnic
COSLA	Convention of Scottish Local Authorities
CPN	Community Psychiatric Nurse
DH	Department of Health (England and Wales)
DHSS	Department of Health and Social Security
DHSSPS	Department of Health, Social Services and Public Safety
DWP	Department for Work and Pensions
ECHR	European Convention on Human Rights
GP	General Practitioner
LASP	Local Adult Safeguarding Partnerships
MHCTSA	Mental Health (Care and Treatment) (Scotland) Act 2003
NIASP	Northern Ireland Adult Safeguarding Partnership
NOI	Northern Ireland Office

INTRODUCTION

> After her death in 2001, a post-mortem found 49 injuries on her body including cuts probably made by a razor blade and cigarette burns. She had moved from sheltered accommodation to her son-in-law's home – five weeks later she was dead. But as the cause of Margaret Panting's death could not be established, no one was ever charged. (House of Commons, 2004)

It has, perhaps, always been somewhat frustrating for many of us in adult care that the perceived procedural clarity of child protection systems are not immediately translated into the protection of adults (Leslie and Pritchard, 2009). However, the right of adults to self-determination (Boyle *et al*, 2002) has, alongside other key issues, meant that the evolution of adult protection has had significant barriers to overcome – in particular the need to ensure that any protective procedures directed at adults did not compromise their human rights (e.g. Article 5 or Article 8 of the European Convention on Human Rights) or extend the state's right to intervene in the rights of adults. It has been increasingly important to acknowledge that, given the catalogue of examples of adults suffering abuse at the hands of others (such as Margaret Panting, above), there is a need to provide protective measures for adults when they could potentially be at risk from harm (Penhale and Parker, 2008). Within this lies the challenge of identifying just what we are protecting adults from as these definitions and thresholds are crucial to the implementation of any policy, guidance or legislation.

The scope of this book
Its principal aim is to examine the existing adult protection framework in the UK, using as a lens theories of citizenship, particularly as they may impact on issues of capacity and choice. The focus is

principally on examining adult support and protection for adults living in the community rather than in residential or institutional settings. Although it should be noted that many of the frameworks considered, e.g the Adult Support and Protection (Scotland) Act 2007, can cover all settings including residential care. *Supporting Vulnerable Adults* takes as an overarching framework the evolution and early implementation of the Adult Support and Protection (Scotland) Act 2007 (ASP) but makes the appropriate links to adult protection policy more broadly in the UK. The focus is specifically on adult protection legislation, policy and guidance and those adults likely to be subject to these systems, but inevitably there will be overlap with broader mental health and incapacity frameworks. However, this volume does not consider those legislative frameworks in detail, because another volume in this series (Atkinson, 2006) provides a discussion of the key elements of the broader civil mental health and incapacity legislation.

The main themes under consideration are the extent of the reach of the state and the appropriateness of this; a discussion of the tension between autonomy and protection; and consideration of whether or not a label of vulnerability and the consequent perceived need for protection impacts on the human and citizenship rights of adults. In addition, concepts of harm and abuse as they relate to adults will be discussed. Key questions considered throughout the book include: does diminished intellectual or physical capacity limit your rights as a citizen; does vulnerability/being at risk of harm and/or abuse equal limited capacity? The book will further explore whether the development and introduction of adult protection procedures and processes can compromise adults' free will and choice inappropriately.

CHAPTER 1

Care vs. Control – The Evolution of Adult Protection in the UK

Introduction

This chapter will consider the evolution of adult protection in the UK and consider the key milestones, including the impact of particular cases as well as the establishment of key organisations, guidance and policy. The emergence of concern about risks to adults living in the community will be considered within a framework of the social construction of risk, harm and abuse. In addition, current data on adults who are deemed to require support and protection in the UK and elsewhere will be explored. Discussion will also take place on the use of language, such as use of the terms safeguarding and vulnerable and, in the Scottish context, support and protection of adults at risk of harm and/or abuse.

Background

Adult Protection in the UK has developed significantly over the last ten years in both policy and legislative terms. Policy, guidance and legislation have been introduced across the four jurisdictions of the UK with increasing regularity. Indeed, it could be argued that never before has the state's reach into the private lives of its citizens been so extended (Stewart, 2011). Consequently, the emerging policy landscape to support this state-sponsored intrusion into the lives of adults (Mackay, 2011) needs to be considered within a framework of the potential for compromising citizenship rights by removing choice.

The evolution of community care and the increasing numbers of adults with support needs living within the community has ensured that the need for effective adult support and protection policy and procedures has become more insistent (Stewart, 2011). For example, between 1980 and 2003, 7,000 people with learning disabilities moved from institutions such as hospitals and multi-occupancy care homes into mainstream communities in Scotland (Scottish Executive, 2004a). However, the history of the support of adults at risk of harm and the state's attempts to prevent harm and afford protection stretches backs much further with perhaps a re-emergence taking place in the 1970s (Scottish Executive, 2007).

Despite this, procedures for adult protection have fallen short of the rigour of child protection across the UK (O'Keefe et al, 2007). However, following a number of high-profile cases across the UK, there have been considerable developments, particularly in the last decade: for example, the introduction of the *No Secrets Guidance* (DH, 2000) in England and *In Safe Hands* (National Assembly for Wales, 2000). The principal focus of adult support and protection at a procedural level focuses on the prevention of harm and/ or abuse. Supporting adults to ensure their own protection either with or without their consent is consequently the core task under consideration.

Awareness of the abuse of adults has been increasing since the middle of the twentieth century: for example, in the 1960s institutional abuse was identified by commentators such as Townsend (1962) and Robb (1967); and in the 1970s by Baker (1975) and Burston (1977). More tellingly, perhaps, in the 1970s and early 1980s, Mervyn Eastman, a social worker, identified from his own caseload that a number of older people living in the community were being harmed by either family members or care professionals and so he raised the profile of the issue in the media. Unfortunately, the tabloid media termed this phenomenon 'granny bashing' (Eastman and Sutton, 1982), which not only, mistakenly, restricted the phenomenon to older people but also labelled the victims as vulnerable. This labelling inferred that the vulnerability was within the individuals themselves rather than the context within which they were harmed, and apportioned blame to the victim.

In the 1980s and 1990s, the pace of work quickened and was taken forward: for example, by Ogg and Bennett (1992) in identifying prevalence rates and through the establishment of Action on Elder Abuse (AEA) in England. Action on Elder Abuse developed a clear campaigning role to raise awareness of the abuse of older people and, consequently, it became more of a political priority – prompting, for example, consideration of policy development in England.

Much activity has taken place since then, often triggered by inquiries into the care and support provided to adults across health and social care: for example, Steven Hoskin – drugged, tortured and forced to fall to his death from a viaduct in Cornwall (BBC, 2008); Kevin Davies – kept like a dog in a locked garden shed before being murdered in Gloucestershire (BBC, 2007a); and Barrie-John Horrell – kidnapped, hit over the head with a brick and strangled in south Wales (BBC, 2007b). These and other inquiries – e.g. Margaret Panting, who five weeks after moving from a care home to her son-in-laws was found dead with more than forty-nine separate injuries (Vickers, 2004) – led to the emergence of an extensive public debate on how to tackle adult protection at a legislative and policy level. Across the UK, guidance to protect adults was initially developed in the 1990s (see, for example, DH, 1993). More recently, revised policy, guidance and legislation have emerged (see, for example, DH, 2000; Scottish Executive, 2001), in response to a number of high-profile community-based incidents of harm being perpetrated against adults: for example, in Cornwall (Commission for Healthcare Audit and Inspection, 2006) and the Scottish Borders (Scottish Executive, 2004b). However, the legislative and procedural framework to support and protect adults at risk of harm has been largely piecemeal and spread across the legal system throughout the UK (see Chapter 2 for further details of legal and policy frameworks). In recognition of the need to develop practice and further measures to protect adults, consultation papers by the English and Scottish law commissions in 1997 laid out recommendations in key areas for policy and legislative reform (see for example Scottish Law Commission, 1997).

To illustrate some of the key challenges in adult protection, a selection of the issues from the Scottish Borders Inquiry (Scottish Executive, 2004b) are highlighted below.

Scottish Borders inquiry – Scottish Executive (2004b)

- failure to investigate appropriately very serious allegations of abuse;
- lack of comprehensive needs assessments or assessment of very poor quality;
- lack of information-sharing and co-ordination between key agencies (including social work, health, education, housing and police);
- very poor standards of case recording, falling well below acceptable practice;
- failure to consider statutory interventions at appropriate stages;
- lack of understanding of the legislative framework for intervention and its capacity to provide protection;
- lack of compliance with procedures;
- failure to understand and balance the issues of self-determination and protection.

The recognition of adult protection as an area of work requiring significant development is, therefore, fairly recent and to some extent is still ill-defined (Mandelstam, 2009). Adult protection is, however, moving forward at considerable pace (Stewart, 2011) with recent reviews of existing policy in both England and Wales as well as the introduction of integrating legislation in Scotland, which will be discussed in detail in Chapter 2.

Language and definitions

The language surrounding adult protection has often been viewed as disempowering and stigmatising: for example, vulnerable, abuse and exploitation (Penhale and Parker, 2008). It is important, therefore, to consider the use of language when referring to adults and the impact this may have on them as well as the way in which it alters perceptions of those individuals: for example, by eroding their rights as citizens.

The term 'safeguarding' is often used with regard to adult protection as it is with the protection of children agenda. It could be argued that, by using parallel language and systems, this infantilises adults as they have the right to self-determination (Boyle *et al*, 2002) in a way that children do not and have capacity (in the main) to make their own decisions (DH, 2009).

During the passage of the primary Scottish legislation, the ASP, much consideration and debate were given to the language contained within it to ensure it did not further stigmatise or disempower adults who may be subject to its powers (MacKay, 2009). Consequently, the language in the legislation became 'adults at risk of harm'; the terms 'abuse' and 'vulnerable' are deliberately avoided, except as part of the definition of 'at risk of harm' (Scottish Government, 2007). There is further, detailed guidance in the legislation and the accompanying code of practice over who could be considered at risk of harm, and this is similar to those considered vulnerable in the Westminster government's *No Secrets Guidance* (DH, 2000). Indeed in the recent consultation to review *No Secrets*, 90% of respondents wanted the definition of vulnerable adults revised and there was significant support for replacing this term with 'person at risk' (DH, 2009). There is a counter-argument, however, which suggests that to reduce what are often criminal acts such as rape, sexual assault, theft or physical assault to one single innocuous term such as 'harm' could trivialise these acts (Brown, 2003). In addition, it has been suggested that 'in an effort to take some of the emotion out of the terminology, the reach arguably extended' (DeSouza, 2011, p. 2).

It is further appropriate to distinguish between those at risk of harm who have capacity and those who lack capacity, because the legislation, policy and procedural frameworks may be significantly different, although there will inevitably be some overlap. In the UK, 'capacity' is a legal term, and thus not only has a legal definition but is also a legal decision (Scottish Government, 2005). There are, for example, specific tests in law that must be carried out to establish capacity where it is in doubt. In Scotland, this will generally be considered within the framework of the Adults with Incapacity (Scotland) Act 2000. Through this legislation a legal decision can be made that an adult lacks capacity to make decisions themselves and empowers someone else to make decisions for them. In England, a similar process exists within the Mental Capacity Act 2005.

Two concepts are, therefore, particularly important to unpack in adult protection – abuse and vulnerability. There are a number of definitions across the UK, perhaps most formally described in the *No Secrets Guidance* (DH, 2000) and the ASP. Examples of definitions from the *No Secrets Guidance* and the ASP are provided below. However, definitions remain a contested area and indeed there has been a suggestion by Bennett, Kingston and Penhale (1997) that we may need different definitions for different areas: for example, for legislation, care management and research.

Defining Abuse

Abuse may consist of a single act or repeated acts. It may be physical, verbal or psychological, it may be an act of neglect or failure to act, or it may occur when a vulnerable person is persuaded to enter into a financial or sexual transaction to which he or she has not consented or cannot give consent.

Abuse can occur in any relationship and may result in significant harm to, or exploitation of, the person subjected to it.

Physical, sexual, financial, emotional, discriminatory or psychological violation or neglect of a person unable to protect him/herself to prevent abuse from happening or to remove him/herself from the abuse of potential abuse by others. (DH, 2000, p. 9)

The ASP defines adults 'at risk' as:

(1) 'Adults at risk' are adults who:

(a) are unable to safeguard their own well-being, property, rights or other interests;

(b) are at risk of harm; and

(c) because they are affected by disability, mental disorder, illness or physical or mental infirmity, are more vulnerable to being harmed than adults who are not so affected.

(2) An adult is at risk of harm for the purposes of subsection (1) if:

(a) another person's conduct is causing (or is likely to cause) the adult to be harmed; or

(b) the adult is engaging (or is likely to engage) in

conduct which causes (or is likely to cause) self-harm. (ASP, 2007, Section 4)

The types of abuse likely to be considered within adult protection are, however, generally agreed on and these include: physical abuse, sexual abuse, psychological abuse, material abuse (such as finance), neglect (including self-neglect), institutional abuse and discriminatory abuse.

Brown (2003, p. 5) argues that the dynamics of abuse are complex and that the factors to be considered include:

- the nature (and underlying intent) of the relationship between the potential abuser and the 'at risk' adult: for example, the process of 'grooming' in respect to a vulnerable adult;
- the process used to gain and maintain access to the vulnerable adult: for example, a perpetrator using the workplace to gain access to 'at risk' adults;
- the degree or severity of the harm to the vulnerable adult (including psychological elements);
- the degree of continuing risk to the vulnerable adult or other 'at risk' adults in the setting: for example, when an accused member of staff continues to have access to the vulnerable adult;
- situations where there might be multiple components of vulnerability: for example, sexual abuse between service users;
- the need to consider the situation where a conflict of interest might occur: for example, where an attorney may be connected to a family member and have their objectivity compromised.

Agreement on what constitutes abuse is, however, unlikely to be universally agreed or to remain static. Abuse is a socially constructed concept and as societies change and evolve so does their understanding and agreement of what is acceptable and unacceptable behaviour, making abuse a fluid concept (Penhale *et al.*, 2000). Therefore, to have a fixed definition of abuse could be detrimental, by essentially classifying certain behaviours as abusive within a constrained set of criteria. In addition, our understanding of abuse and abusive behaviour is likely to be affected by local and cultural factors, including existing practice and procedures and, consequently, a range of definitions are inevitable (Penhale *et al*, 2000). It is, therefore, important when con-

sidering whether or not abuse is present and if an adult requires protection that the definition of abuse and/or harm being used is explicit,
either legislatively or procedurally (Stewart, 2011).

Consequently, the adults most likely to be subject to the protection
afforded by the policy and statute discussed within this volume are
those who have experienced or who are at risk from some form of
abuse/exploitation or harm either by themselves or by external influences and who are living in a range of settings.

Prevalence rates

Perhaps one of the reasons for the slow-moving policy response to
adult protection has been the challenge in establishing prevalence rates
(Stewart, 2011). In common with other protection agendas, harm
perpetrated against adults often goes unreported because of the fear
of recrimination and concern about being abandoned (Penhale and
Parker, 2008). Prevalence rates are consequently difficult to establish
and there is little robust evidence about the extent of the abuse of
adults in the UK (Pritchard, 2009). In addition, the limited work that
has been carried out to establish prevalence has, in the main, focused
on older people (see for example O'Keefe *et al*, 2007); very little is
known formally about levels of harm, abuse and exploitation amongst
other adults potentially at risk such as those with learning disabilities
or those experiencing mental disorder.

Comic Relief and the DH funded a two-year study undertaken by
Kings College, London and the National Centre for Social Research
(O'Keefe *et al.*, 2007), which provides some evidence of prevalence rates
of harm amongst older adults. This study found that 4% of older adults
in the UK are victims of elder abuse, amounting to 342,000 people and
that 2.6% were abused by people considered to be in a position of trust
including family members, neighbours and health and social care staff.
However, the detail of what constitutes abuse is contested and there is
no agreement on a single definition (McCreadie, 1996). This lack of a
clear definition is likely to impact on the accuracy of prevalence rates
if the parameters used to define the phenomenon vary considerably.
Penhale (1993) argues that despite this lack of agreed definition there
is general consensus on the most common types of abuse. Phillipson
and Biggs (1995, p. 202) further note that:

Attempts to define and map the extent of elder abuse indicate that it should not be seen as a single monolithic phenomenon, but that it takes a variety of forms in different settings and in different kinds of relationships.

The types of abuse perpetrated in the above study were found to include: neglect – 105,000; financial – 86,500; psychological – 58,600; physical – 62,400; sexual – 42,000 (O'Keefe *et al*, 2007). Whilst this study was limited to older adults, it does provide some baseline data on the types of harm perpetrated more generally.

Victims of harm were identified as predominantly women. In addition, those who lived alone were found to be more likely to experience neglect; those who were lonely, had poor health or a poor quality of life were more likely to experience abuse. Partners, family members and neighbours were found to be the most likely abusers, followed by care workers and friends (O"Keefe, 2007).

Cooper *et al.* (2008) carried out a systematic review of elder abuse and neglect that covered forty-nine studies from across the world. This review found that 6% of older people reported significant abuse in the last month and 5% of couples reported physical violence in their relationship. Rates of abuse were reported at a similar level to that found in the UK study. In addition, categories of abuse were similar: for example, psychological, physical and financial. Perhaps, more importantly, Cooper *et al.* (2008) conclude that of the one in four older people at risk of abuse only a small proportion were currently detected. They further found that the older people and their caregivers both formal and informal were willing to report abuse and felt that they should be asked about this routinely.

Why protect adults?
As can be seen from the above discussion, unpacking the concept of adult protection requires consideration of a range of issues, including the social construction of risk, harm and abuse. What do adults at risk of harm look like and what are they at risk from? How do we begin to consider what factors warrant/merit intervention in the life of an adult, with capacity or without? What factors allows society to intervene in the personal lives of its citizens? What makes some

adults more vulnerable to harm than others? Perhaps the simplest way to approach this is through illustration.

Assessing the seriousness of situations prior to intervention is at the core of practice in the support and protection of adults at risk of harm as with other areas of health and social work practice. Assessing seriousness is, perhaps, most closely linked to the concept of significant harm (Stewart, 2011). Significant harm is an important concept as it aids practitioners in determining how serious or extensive abuse must be to warrant intervention (O'Keefe *et al.*, 2007). There are, perhaps, helpful parallels with child protection where significant harm, introduced in the Children Act 1989, is viewed as the threshold after which compulsory intervention is required. The Law Commission in England (1995) makes use of this concept when considering the nature of intervention and defines this as including not only ill treatment but also impeding and impairing the development of an adult in a number of areas including physical and emotional. Deciding on an intervention may further require consideration of the degree, extent, duration and frequency of harm (Mandelstam, 2009).

In addition, it is important to define adult protection as broader than physical or sexual abuse, so that it also includes psychological and financial abuse and exploitation (Mantell and Scragg, 2008). The harm that can be perpetuated against an adult can fall into a number of categories, although O'Keefe *et al.* (2007) found overlapping issues with significant complexity and that where abuse existed it was often incremental.

A further consideration is why people harm adults. A range of triggers have been identified within the *No Secrets Guidance* in England (DH, 2000) including:

- opportunistic – money, valuables lying around in plain sight;
- long-term – history of abuse, harm within family or situation;
- situational – pressure built up over time, e.g. long-term care;
- neglect – withholding of appropriate care;
- unacceptable treatment – punishment for specific behaviours.

Many factors that trigger adults being harmed are similar to those in child abuse, particularly as they relate to situational and opportunistic triggers. The examples provided below illustrate what form the abuse can take and the impact of this on adults.

EXAMPLE 1

Ms B has a mild to moderate learning disability. She lived in a hostel for homeless people for a number of years during which time she was subjected to a significant number of physical and sexual assaults (more than twenty), was often absent overnight and was often found to have no money for food. She was resistant to additional support being provided or having the perceived abuse addressed. Ms B had on a number of occasions reported the abuse to the police as well as hostel staff but always recanted her testimony.

Hostel staff consistently expressed concerns that Ms B was being financially, physically and sexually abused and that over time the level and frequency of abuse were increasing. She often returned to the company of a 'friend' who had been present at and participated in a number of assaults perpetrated against her.

EXAMPLE 2

John Davidson is a retired architect who lives in a rural area; he is frail physically but cognitively very sharp and aware. His son and daughter-in-law live with him. John also has two other daughters. John's son and daughter-in-law do not work, neither do they claim benefits; consequently, their income is derived solely from John. One of John's daughters has written to the social work department to raise concerns that her father is being financially exploited by her brother and his wife. Staff from the local social work department interviewed John and it became clear that he was frustrated with his son. John has challenged his son about claiming benefits and/or working, but his son refuses to claim benefits, saying it is beneath him and his wife. He also argues that there are no jobs available. John has asked both his son and daughter-in-law to leave as he feels they are a drain on him financially and emotionally or to secure their own income.

The above clearly illustrate the challenges of the different elements of abuse from financial, physical and sexual in example 1 to psychological and financial in example 2.

Vulnerability

Vulnerability is a term often used to describe those who require support to ensure their own protection. However, all adults could be considered vulnerable at some stage in their adult life (Beckett, 2006). Indeed, vulnerability (and what determines it) is itself a contentious concept (Penhale and Parker, 2008). Attributing a label of vulnerable to an individual can consign them to the status of victim, having things done to them rather than helping themselves, for example. In addition, the term 'vulnerable adult' can instil the vulnerability within the adult himself or herself, rather than the vulnerability being caused by a particular set of circumstances or particular context (Penhale and Parker, 2008). In this sense, vulnerable adults can be viewed through the same lens as other marginalised groups whose label has disempowered them (Stewart, 2011).

There are, further, often conflicting views concerning an individual's capacity and social situation, which may aid in defining vulnerability. It can often be an adult's context, which means that he or she is at risk of harm and, consequently, deemed vulnerable: for example, he or she may be living with someone who is exploiting them financially (see Example 2, above) and if that person were removed they would no longer be deemed at risk or vulnerable. The *No Secrets* (DH, 2000, p. 9) guidance suggests that:

> A vulnerable adult is a person aged eighteen years or over who is or may be in need of community care services by reason of mental or other disability, age or illness; and who is or may be unable to take care of him or herself, or unable to protect him or herself against significant harm or exploitation.

The guidance goes on to indicate that those adults falling into the above category must be considered on a case-by-case basis as their own situation and context may impact on any decisions regarding intervention.

This book, in the main, uses the terms 'adult support and protection' and 'adults at risk of harm' as these are viewed as the least stigmatising and most empowering for service users (Stewart, 2011).

Policy and legislative frameworks across the UK

The complexity of adult protection signifies that any legislative or policy responses must be flexible, provide a range of detailed responses and be understood across health, social care, education and justice agencies (Scottish Executive, 2007). Local authorities have a clear lead in adult support and protection across the UK, although the details of this vary across the four jurisdictions within the UK. This, inevitably, means that social workers in particular are required to balance complex ethical and practice dilemmas within frameworks that rely heavily on inter-agency collaboration to ensure effective outcomes for adults.

The range of legal and procedural measures available to support and protect adults at risk of harm is viewed as considerable, but they are spread across different areas of law, such as criminal justice, social care and education (Scottish Executive, 2007). It is important to recognise that there is no consolidating piece of legislation in England, Wales or Northern Ireland, which protects adults deemed at risk of harm (MacKay, 2011).

Finally it is important to establish what the aim of the legislation or policy is (such as, to treat, support or protect) when considering how best it could be used or how effective it might be (Scottish Executive, 2007).

Joint working

The importance of effective joint working particularly across health and social care and justice agencies is emphasised across all policy guidance in the UK and more broadly (see, for example, DH, 2000). Often the first person to identify an adult at risk of harm will be a home care worker or health professional (O'Keefe *et al.*, 2007), or the police may be notified due to concerns of neighbours. It is imperative, therefore, that where concerns are identified that relevant agencies (most likely local authorities who have lead responsibility) are notified.

Context

The nature of situations that require adults to be supported and/or protected are likely to be complex, with rapidly shifting parameters which needs fluid, flexible statutory approaches. This requires that practitioners working within adult protection are able to respond quickly to rapidly deteriorating or indeed improving situations to ensure that adults are neither overly monitored nor constrained in living their lives within the community (Stewart, 2011). Effective case and care management procedures as well as effective integrated working across health, social care, police and education are likely to be at the core of effective practice. (Hogg et al, 2009a)

As citizens of the UK we expect to be able to live our lives in a way that we want, even if our neighbours do not view that as appropriate. For example, if I wish to value the friendship of an individual above the fact that they take money from me or occasionally are physically violent towards me, is that my decision to make? Or, should I expect and wish society to protect me from decisions that are likely to cause me harm? Adult protection procedures in whatever form must straddle this difficult line between care and control, autonomy and protection.

Clearly, the prevailing culture is that those adults deemed at risk of harm and, consequently, considered vulnerable are those defined in law or by policy as being unable to protect themselves from harm without support. These policies and laws are likely to draw on the social construction of risk, vulnerability and abuse for these definitions. In the UK, for example, this is likely to include those who are in receipt of some form of statutory service or brought to the attention of statutory services and deemed unable to protect themselves because of illness, mental/physical disability or age (Scottish Executive, 2007). These features further emphasise the need for effective joint working.

Conclusion

The foregoing has provided an overview of the emergence of adult protection as an issue in the UK as well as a brief discussion of some of the key concepts and challenges in this field of social policy and practice. The social construction of a number of the key concepts, particularly vulnerability and abuse, inevitably mean that approaches to adult protection are likely to be fluid and to change over time and cultures depending on the prevailing social norms.

The challenge of ensuring that control does not outweigh care, that autonomy is not inappropriately sacrificed in favour of protection and that choice and decision-making remain where possible with the adult themselves is at the core of adult protection policy. Maintaining that balance is likely, therefore, to be in the interpretation and implementation of guidance, policy and legislation; and as such is the purview of health, social care and justice organisations and their staff across the UK and more broadly demanding effective joint working.

Divergence for Better or Worse? – Adult Support and Protection in the UK in the Twenty-First Century

Introduction

The following chapter aims broadly to plot the key elements of the various adult protection systems across the UK. This will include details of the *No Secrets* policy framework in England (DH, 2000), *In Safe Hands* in Wales (National Assembly for Wales, 2000), the ASP in Scotland and the vulnerable adults guidance in Northern Ireland (Northern Ireland Social Services Board, 2006). Chapter 2 will further consider some of the themes arising from the *No Secrets* review in England (DH, 2009) and link this to the broader research literature on adults considered to be at risk of harm. These themes include choice and control, links to other policy developments such as personalisation and the concept of criminalising abuse such as financial exploitation as theft and physical abuse as assault. A central consideration in this chapter will be whether or not legislation is actually required to ensure the support and protection of adults, and a discussion is provided on the benefits and challenges of introducing such legislation.

Although policy and legislation surrounding adult protection has evolved significantly over the last ten years, particularly across the UK, the frameworks that have developed appear quite different across the four jurisdictions of the UK, often depending on government priority, ideology and the particular focus of high-profile cases (MacKay, 2011). In addition, the focus of protection systems across the UK has, it could be argued, depended greatly on the reasons for its development. In Scotland, the focus of the legislation and the protective measures available are grounded in the protection of individuals' rights (Northern Ireland Assembly, 2008) and based on a series of principles including benefit, participation and the least restrictive alternative. This is true across the triangle of protection in Scotland, which includes the Mental Health (Care and Treatment) (Scotland) Act 2003 and the Adults with Incapacity (Scotland) Act 2000 (MacKay, 2008). However, in England, Pilgrim (2007) suggests that the legislative system available to protect adults is based on the notion of public safety rather than simply the safety of the adult. MacKay (2011) further suggests that whilst this variance is not uncommon across other European countries the fact that this disparity is taking place within the UK, where broadly similar patterns of reform in mental health law have taken place, is significant. This fundamental difference in approach to the notion of adult support and protection and the diverging political landscape in the UK ensures that, whilst the systems have broadly similar aims, the underlying principles may differ. Whether or not this makes a significant difference to outcomes for adults within the system is beyond the scope of this volume.

Policy overview

Whilst there may arguably be fundamentally different approaches to adult protection across the four jurisdictions in the UK, there are also many common elements. These include procedural guidance for staff undertaking investigations into adult protection; the need for effective joint working between the key agencies; definitions of harm and/or abuse; as well as consideration of thresholds for formal intervention in the life of an adult.

The following provides a brief overview of the key elements of each of the policies/guidance.

Scotland

Here there is specific primary legislation, the Adult Support and Protection (Scotland) Act 2007 (ASP), to cover those who require support and protection as they are deemed at risk of harm. This legislation importantly places a duty on local authorities and their key

partners – health boards, police, education and voluntary organisations – to work together to support and protect adults at risk of
harm. The legislation is also based on a set of principles which aims
to provide the means to intervene and prevent harm continuing and
the framework to put in place strengthened measures to give greater
protection for those at risk from harm and to improve inter-agency
co-operation and promote good inter-disciplinary practice.

However, the ASP is only one part of a legal structure that provides
the framework for inquiry, assessment and intervention in the lives of
adults in Scotland. The Mental Health (Care and Treatment) (Scotland) Act 2003 (MHCTSA) and the Adults with Incapacity (Scotland)
Act 2000 (AWIA) are the other two key elements. The AWIA provides
for the support and protection of those adults who lack capacity and
the MHCT Act provides for the support and protection of those who
are experiencing mental disorder.

The ASP introduced new adult support and protection powers and
procedures to protect adults at risk of harm and to support them to
more effectively protect themselves. Adults at risk of harm are defined
as those who are affected by illness, mental disorder, disability, infirmity or ageing and as a result are at risk of harm (Section 3 of the ASP,
2007). It further established multi-agency adult protection committees to oversee strategic and operational effectiveness of prevention
and protection interventions.

In addition to the creation of adult protection committees, the key
elements of ASP:

- place a duty on a range of agencies to investigate suspected
  abuse;
- provide new powers to carry out assessments of the person and
  their circumstances, in private where necessary;
- create a range of options for intervention to address and
  manage instances of abuse;
- require that intervention under the Act must benefit the adult
  and be the least restrictive option.

The specific powers available for use under the ASP are:

- to investigate suspected harm;
- to carry out assessments of the adult and their circumstances;
- to intervene to remove the adult or manage the risk of harm;

- if necessary and as a last resort, to exclude the perpetrator – banning orders;
- if necessary and as a last resort, to force entry to perform the above functions.

Importantly, in line with the other jurisdictions, a key element of the Scottish framework is that the service users consent should underpin any measures adopted: for example, none of the above powers should be utilised without the consent of the adult. However, Section 35 does allow for overriding the consent of the adult, with the agreement of a sheriff, if there appears to be undue pressure being applied to the adult by an external source (for example, the perpetrator of the suspected abuse and/or harm) to withhold their consent. There are no publicly available figures to illustrate to what extent orders have been granted without the consent of the adult, but, anecdotally, it appears to be very low.

The issue of undue pressure and the necessary evidence to prove undue pressure (for which the sheriff must hold a reasonable belief that the adult is being prevented from giving their consent) (Calder, 2010) is a contentious one and largely, to date, untested in law. Smith and Patrick (2009) argue that any adult being subject to an order granted under this legislation without their consent may be able to contend that their right to a private life has been infringed and that, depending on how the order was exercised, it could potentially constitute an unlawful deprivation of liberty under Article 5 of the European Convention on Human Rights (ECHR).

England

In 2000, the Westminster government launched the *No Secrets Guidance* (DH, 2000), which aimed to provide a clear policy framework for adult protection in England. This included a focus on the development of inter-agency policies and procedures to protect adults at risk of harm. In addition, it offered a structure for the development of local policies and procedures as well as joint protocols. It did not, however, place a statutory duty on agencies to comply with the guidance, although there was an expectation that, unless there were very clear reasons for exemption, all relevant agencies would do so. The guidance provides details on a range of issues for practitioners and agencies including: definitions of abuse; an explanation of how and why abuse occurs, including patterns of abuse; how to respond to various kinds of abuse; consideration of what level of abuse justifies intervention; and the development of inter-agency protocols.

Further to the production of the *No Secrets Guidance* in 2000, the Association of Directors of Social Services (ADSS) – now the Association of Directors of Adult Social Services (ADASS) – produced *Safeguarding Adults* guidance (ADSS, 2005) to further clarify practice in adult protection. The guidance is presented as a framework of good practice standards, which address issues such as accountability and the responsibilities of partner agencies.

In 2008–9, in response to concerns about a lack of clarity in the *No Secrets* policy (DH, 2000), the Department of Health reviewed the guidance in consultation with key stakeholders. Included amongst the recommendations for change in the final report are that:

- safeguarding should be built on empowerment; without this, it is experienced as safety at the expense of other qualities of life, such as self-determination and the right to family life;
- individuals should be empowered, and safeguarding decisions should be taken by the individual concerned. While people wanted help with options, information and support, they still wanted to retain control and make their own choices;
- safeguarding adults is not like child protection; adults do not want to be treated like children and do not want a system that was designed for children;
- the participation/representation of people who lack capacity is also important (DH, 2009).

More recently (January 2010), Phil Hope, the then Care Minister in England, detailed the government's response to the review of *No Secrets* indicating amongst other measures that safeguarding boards would be made mandatory throughout England, further emphasising the importance of adult protection in both policy and practice terms.

Wales

The policy developed in Wales to support and protect adults at risk of harm is entitled *In Safe Hands* (National Assembly for Wales,

2000). *In Safe Hands* was issued as guidance in 2000 under Section 7 of the Local Authority Social Services Act 1970. The focus of this policy is on effective inter-agency working and information sharing in particular. Further guidance on the protection of vulnerable adults from financial abuse in their own homes was developed in 2003 and updated in 2009. More detailed information on adult protection in Wales can be found at URL: www.ssiacymru.org.uk/index.cfm?articleid=2592 (accessed 11 July 2011).

As with the other jurisdictions within the UK, the implementation of the Welsh policy has not been without its challenges. In June 2009, for example, Gary Fitzgerald, Chief Executive of the charity Action on Elder Abuse stated that he felt the impact of the policy 'was an illusion not a reality' and that it had failed to protect older people (Western Mail, June 2009). This concern focused on the fact that the policy did not carry the same weight as legislation and that, as such, local authorities could ignore the guidance with good reason. As with the review of *No Secrets* in England, campaigners called for a broad review of the Welsh policy, which took place in 2009–10, undertaken by the Welsh Institute of Health and Social Care, University of Glamorgan (Magill et al, 2010). The report concluded that *In Safe Hands* has been only partially effective. It was felt not to have met the needs of more marginalised groups such as those from black and minority ethnic (BME) communities, that elements of it were no longer appropriate (such as the title was felt to indicate recipients of support and protection were passive) and that it had not been particularly robust (particularly with regard to the promotion of inter-agency working) (Magill *et al*, 2010). In order to combat these concerns, sixteen recommendations were agreed. These included:

- principles of safeguarding – key principles were developed to underpin the provision of support and protection of adults at risk of harm in Wales. These included: taking the wishes of the adult into account; ensuring that actions taken have the consent of the adult; priority being given to stop abuse continuing whilst recognising the balance to be struck between autonomy and protection;
- legislation – it was agreed that legislation was required and that it should, amongst other things, define who should be covered

by the act; it should also promote inter-agency collaboration via a statutory framework and create a new offence of ill-treatment or neglect of an adult with capacity;

- sanctions – as the majority of respondents favoured some form of sanction, further consultation was considered appropriate to examine the range and scope of possible sanctions;
- raising awareness – it was recognised that a major publicity campaign was required to raise awareness of the issue of adult protection. A focus of the campaign was to ensure adults themselves were aware they should expect protection from abuse and how to ensure they got it. (Magill, 2010)

Further details on the outcome of the review can be found at URL: http://wales.gov.uk/docs.dhss/publications/100914insafehandsrevi ewen.pdf (accessed 11 July 2011).

Northern Ireland

The policy document *Safeguarding Vulnerable Adults: Regional Adult Protection and Policy Procedural Guidance* (Northern Ireland Social Services Board, 2006) lays out the framework for adult protection in Northern Ireland. This includes discussion of definitions, principles and the importance of inter-agency working. Recent developments have included the *Protocol for Joint Investigation of Alleged and Suspected Cases of Abuse of Vulnerable Adults* by the Regional Adult Protection Forum (2009), which is a partnership body, with representation from Health and Social Care Trusts and Board, Police Service for Northern Ireland, the Regulation and Quality Improvement Authority and the voluntary sector. It outlines roles and responsibilities of the respective agencies and provides guidance about joint working arrangements and investigation.

As with other jurisdictions in the UK, this policy has been subject to review. *Reforming Northern Ireland's Adult Protection Infrastructure*, produced by the Department of Health, Social Services and Public Safety (DHSSPS, 2009) and the Northern Ireland Office (NIO), with the support of other government departments was issued in November 2009. Following the consultation, the establishment of a new Northern Ireland Adult Safeguarding Partnership (NIASP) and five Local Adult Safeguarding Partnerships (LASP) was announced. Work to date has focused on establishing the NIASP and the LASPs as well as creating appropriate links with other jurisdictions. A rights-based, multi-disciplinary, inter-agency approach to adult safeguarding will be taken by the new partnership.

In addition to the above, good practice guidance entitled *Safeguarding Vulnerable Adults – A Shared Responsibility* has been launched (Volunteer Now, 2010). It sets out eight key safeguarding standards and criteria to achieve those standards as well as helpful resources. The eight standards are:

- The organisation has a safeguarding vulnerable adults policy supported by robust procedures.
- The organisation consistently applies a thorough and clearly defined method of recruiting staff and volunteers in line with legislative requirements and best practice.
- There are procedures in place for the effective management, support, supervision and training of staff and volunteers.
- The organisation has clearly defined procedures for raising awareness of, responding to, and recording and reporting concerns about actual or suspected incidents of abuse.
- The organisation operates an effective procedure for assessing and managing risks with regard to safeguarding vulnerable adults.
- There are clear procedures for receiving comments and suggestions and for dealing with concerns and complaints about the organisation.
- The organisation has a clear policy on the management of records, confidentiality and sharing of information.
- There is a written code that outlines the behaviour expected of all involved with the organisation, including visitors.
  (Volunteer Now, 2010, Section 2)

The Volunteer Now (2010) guidance was funded by the DHSSPS and developed by Volunteer Now in consultation with a Safeguarding Vulnerable Adults Advisory Group. A full copy of the guidance can be downloaded from the Volunteer Now website at URL: www. volunteernow.co.uk/fs/doc/publications/safeguarding-vulnerable-adults-a-shared-responsibility-colour-nl.pdf (accessed March 2011). These changes to the policy framework within Northern Ireland are taking place within the context of the potential development of a single unifying piece of legislation for those likely to be subject to mental incapacity and mental health legislation described within the Bamford Report (DHSSPS, 2007).

Reviewing effectiveness in adult protection

As the Scottish legislation has been implemented for just over three years it has not yet been reviewed or evaluated by the Scottish Government, although the literature does highlight some potential concerns with this system to date (see, for example, MacKay, 2008). Indeed, the empirical research discussed in more detail in Chapters 3 and 5 of this book is some of the earliest work carried out on the implementation of this Act. A number of local authorities are, however, undertaking their own local evaluations and these are likely to be published during late 2011 or early 2012.

Some of the key themes raised prior to implementation of the ASP were related to whether or not the legislation would empower or disempower adults at risk of harm, particularly in the community (MacKay, 2008). Discussion focused on whether by providing the opportunity to override consent there was a danger of protection overriding autonomy and control denying choice for adults. This was of particular concern as the expectation was that, in the main, those adults subject to the powers of the ASP would be deemed to have capacity to make decisions for themselves. The issue of capacity, the ASP and adult protection is an area that will be further explored in Chapter 4.

As earlier identified, the *No Secrets Guidance* (DH, 2000) in England was reviewed in 2008–9 and consulted on widely. In a general sense, there was a view that *Safeguarding Adults* (DH, 2009) should focus on care and support as well as preventative work, rather than concentrating solely on protection, already a key element of the Scottish legislation. The report following the consultation and the government's response to it was published in July 2009 and raised a number of key issues under the following general themes (DH, 2009):

- There was concern over the potential link between adults at risk of harm and the implementation of the personalisation agenda. Concern was expressed that those individuals who may be at risk of harm would be doubly disadvantaged within a personalised framework, particularly where they were managing direct payments. Opportunities for financial abuse were seen to be significant where those at risk of harm had direct payments or individual budgets to secure their support.

- The use of the term 'vulnerable' was viewed as problematic and stigmatising. The argument was posited that adults are not intrinsically vulnerable but that their context or situation can make them so and that vulnerability will change over time as situations change. Some considerable support was expressed for changing the term 'vulnerable' to 'adult at risk' (90% of respondents) during the review. In addition, there was some concern about labelling carers as perpetrators or using the term abuse when caring responsibilities became overwhelming and what was required was additional support rather than punitive measures taken against carers as well as labelling them as abusers. These issues are discussed in more detail as they relate to the evolution and implementation of the ASP in Chapters 3 and 5.

- Mechanisms that ensured an appropriate balance between autonomy and protection were considered key – many service users indicating that whilst they wanted support they needed to maintain the right to make those decisions for themselves.

- A view was expressed that there was a need to develop further the agenda in the NHS. The key concern here was the lack of ownership of this agenda in the health services.

- A key role for local adult protection committees should be on ensuring effective inter-agency collaboration, particularly in terms of communication and information sharing. This reflects the issues previously identified with regard to sharing of information between the key agencies, and the consequences of this lack of co-operation have been apparent in a number of high-profile cases (see, for example, Stewart, 2008)

- There was widespread support (68% of respondents) for legislation focusing on adult protection, for a number of reasons, including the need to balance choice and safeguarding, making adult protection a priority and that the protection of adults should mirror child protection to a degree. However, in contrast, reasons given for not promoting legislation as a response to some of the issues in the review were: that much had been achieved without legislation; that it would not necessarily make adult protection a priority; that the experience in Scotland would need to be evaluated over a number of years; and finally that the protection agenda should be part of the mainstream choice agenda.

It is difficult to balance some of these concerns with the need to provide adults with protection. In addition, there is a need to consider further the links to criminal justice for issues such as theft, sexual assault, domestic violence and assault. Adult protection should not be used to excuse or minimise the abuse of adults where they should be categorised as criminal offences or indeed be seen as the soft option when dealing with perpetrators.

Divergence – positive or negative?

An increasing divergence has, as can be noted above, developed in adult protection frameworks between Scotland and the rest of the UK (MacKay, 2009). Much has been made of the consolidating nature of the ASP legislation in Scotland and the contrasting disadvantages of the disparate nature of the legislation and policy drawn on in England, Wales and Northern Ireland: for example, limited use of possible measures owing to lack of knowledge amongst practitioners (Hewitt, 2009). Perhaps, however, one of the advantages of having no consolidating legislation in England, Wales and Northern Ireland is that practitioners are empowered to act by more than one piece of legislation such as: Section 47 of the NHS and Community Care Act 1990; and Sections 29 and 47 of the National Assistance Act 1948. These myriad options could promote innovative practice models.

Many practitioners will have used Section 47 of the National Assistance Act 1948, which allows for the removal of someone at risk of harm and to confine them in a more suitable place. However, there are challenges in using this tool for protection in that, although it is there to ensure a person receives appropriate and necessary care and attention, it is perhaps less specific than the newly developed guidance. Some may argue, however, that it could be used more flexibly. There is, further, little detail available about how effectively this statute supports and protects those at risk of harm, although there is some information on the number of orders made: for example, 165 orders were made between 1988 and 1991 (Nair and Mayberry, 1995).

In addition, practitioners in England have been able to use aspects of the Race Relations Act 1976, Disability Discrimination Act 2005 and the Human Rights Act 1998 in various forms to support and protect adults at risk of harm. Hewitt (2009, p. 30), however, suggests that: 'a wide variety of safeguarding powers already exists. If some of them are little used, that may be because they are in unfamiliar places.' This further indicates that the lack of a consolidating piece of legislation may be impacting on practice.

Prior to the implementation of the ASP in Scotland similar issues were identified. A review, for example, of the published inquiries undertaken by the Mental Welfare Commission in Scotland to establish common themes (Stewart, 2008) found that one of the key elements in each of the inquiries was a lack of knowledge amongst practitioners with regard to the most effective use of existing legislation to promote protection and a lack of support locally to find the relevant information. Perhaps, therefore, consolidating the focus into integrated policy or legislative frameworks will ensure that relevant staff will become familiar with the procedures they require to use to work effectively with adults at risk of harm.

Nonetheless, the clear disadvantage of the above is that these frameworks are fragmented, inconsistently applied and overall unclear (Stewart, 2011). Some 68% of those who responded to the written consultation on the review of the English *No Secrets Guidance* (DH, 2000) supported the need to develop legislation – the reasons for this were that:

- safeguarding adults should be given the same priority as child protection;
- legislation would make safeguarding a priority;
- Scotland has the ASP, which made adult protection statutory;
- the government's choice agenda needed to be balanced with a safeguarding agenda (DH, 2009).

There are a number of other areas that require consideration within the divergent policy frameworks; including inter-agency collaboration, and the extent of the reach of the state.

A number of the policy documents and legislation cited above have as their central aim the co-ordination of effective systems across agencies to best support and protect adults at risk of harm with associated codes of practice and local arrangements providing procedural clarity for practitioners. The *Mental Welfare Commission for Scotland* report on common themes in published inquiries found that one of the main reasons for adults slipping through the existing net of protection was the lack of appropriate co-ordination and information sharing between the key agencies involved (Stewart, 2008). Key elements of the ASP in Scotland compel co-ordination between a range of agencies to protect adults at risk of harm, such as in the establishment of multi-agency adult protection committees. The recent reviews of the adult protection policies in the other UK jurisdictions have recommended similar measures to ensure more effective inter-agency collaboration (see for example DH, 2009).

A number of the key themes, which arose in the review of *No Secrets* (DH, 2009), highlight and reflect inherent ethical concerns in the extent of the role of society to protect people who for a variety of defined reasons are unable to protect themselves or even to acknowledge that they require help. The requirement, for example, for consent (DH, 2009) to intervene under the legislation and/or policy would indicate that we as a society are uncomfortable with the notion that adults (very much like ourselves) could be subject to what could be considered, particularly in the Scottish context, fairly extraordinary powers, such as being removed from your own home for the purposes of assessment (ASP, 2007) or having a member of your family banned from your own home or from contact in your day-to-day life (ASP, 2007). Indeed, the *No Secrets* review (DH, 2009) finds that a key message from the participation of older people, adults with learning or other disabilities and people with mental health problems was that:

> safeguarding must be built on empowerment – or listening to the victim's voice. Without this, safeguarding is

experienced as safety at the expense of other qualities of life, such as self-determination and the right to family life. (DH, 2009, p. 5)

This section of the review goes on to highlight that it is everyone's responsibility to ensure that individuals are empowered to make safeguarding decisions for themselves. Whilst adults want to be presented with options, information and support, they also want to retain control for themselves and make their own choices (DH, 2009). This reflects the underlying principles of the ASP in Scotland. It could be argued therefore that the opportunity for overriding consent within the ASP where undue pressure can be evidenced could undermine the adult's right to self-determination (Boyle *et al*, 2002).

Personalisation and adult protection – friend or foe?
The personalisation agenda in the UK has developed from the campaigning of the disability movement for greater choice and control for service users over the supports they receive. Personalisation aims to ensure that every person who receives support, whether provided by the statutory sector, the independent (such as voluntary or private) sector or funded by themselves is empowered to shape their own lives and the supports they receive in all care settings (Demos, 2004). In Scotland, personalisation has largely focused on the development of Self-Directed Support (see, for example, Scottish Government, 2011). How does this chime, therefore, with adult protection and the need to enforce protective measures on to adults? The DH review (2009) finds that there was concern that the balance between personalisation and the protection of adults had not yet been realised. Furthermore, this balance of choice and risk had not yet been determined and that, despite some good work around the delivery of both adult protection and personalisation, additional work was needed to develop financial safeguarding in the light of the developments on personalisation. The links between risk, personalisation, vulnerability and adult protection are discussed in more detail in Chapter 5.

Conclusion

There appears to be general consensus from the English and Welsh reviews about the key areas for development and/or concern with regard to existing policy, guidance and legislation. In general, these can be summarised as: the balance between autonomy and protection; the use of language, making links to broader agendas in particular personalisation; and the promotion of more effective inter-agency collaboration. However, none of the other jurisdictions is currently following Scotland's lead and developing a legislative approach to adult protection. Largely, it appears that this is because of the current lack of evidence on whether or not this is actually required to achieve effective outcomes for service users and carers.

Whilst the adult protection frameworks across the UK seem to be diverging in terms of the need for specific legislation, what appears to be emerging are that similar areas for concern/development remain across the systems. Perhaps not unsurprisingly at the core of these concerns is the balance between autonomy and protection. This is a difficult balance to achieve and the following chapters will consider some of the approaches that might be taken, using the ASP as illustration as well as consideration of the ongoing challenges in developing adult protection. In addition, the contemporary political direction of travel in the UK for the care and support of all citizens appears to be based on participation and co-production. A shift in responsibility, therefore, from the state to the individual appears to be the likely outcome (Ferguson, 2007). Whether or not this supports or challenges the adult support and protection agenda will be discussed later in this volume.

CHAPTER 3

How Did We Get Here? – The Evolution of the Adult Support and Protection (Scotland) Act 2007

Introduction

The focus of this chapter is to consider the evolution of the Adult Support and Protection (Scotland) Act 2007 and the key issues and concepts discussed during its development. In examining the evolution of the primary legislation in Scotland, this chapter will consider emerging findings from empirical research. This research aims to examine theories of citizenship, capacity and choice using as an overarching framework, the development and early implementation of the ASP as well as the broader academic literature.

The ASP is, arguably, one of the few pieces of legislation in the world designed to protect and support adults both within and outwith a specific mental health or incapacity framework (MacKay, 2009). Whilst the ASP does include in its definition of 'at risk of harm' those affected by mental disorder and mental infirmity, it also covers those 'made more vulnerable by disability, illness and physical infirmity' (ASP, 2007). Therefore, implicitly, it is likely to impact on the lives of adults who neither lack capacity nor are experiencing mental disorder. This legislated intervention into the lives of adults who have capacity and the right to self-determination is a significant departure from the approach taken in other parts of the UK and Europe (MacKay, 2011). Recent reviews of adult protection policies in England and Wales have highlighted the demand for legislation to be developed in other parts of the UK (DH, 2009; Welsh Institute for Health and Social Care, 2010). Is this demand premature given the early stage of implementation of the legislation in Scotland? It is unclear, for example, at this stage whether outcomes for adults will improve through the use of the legislation.

The detail of the individual powers and duties of the ASP are discussed in Chapter 2 so they will not be repeated in detail here. However, it is important to acknowledge that the ASP introduces new adult protection powers and duties to protect adults at risk of harm. The Act replaces Section 47 of the National Assistance Act 1948 and includes action to prevent self-neglect/self-harm. Existing Scottish legislation can be used to protect a person from harm or exploitation – for example, Adults with Incapacity (Scotland) Act 2000 and the Mental Health (Care and Treatment) (Scotland) Act 2003 – but only if they have a mental disorder and/or lack capacity and meet the appropriate legislative tests. Therefore, the ASP aims to protect those who fall outwith the legal tests for support and protection or care and treatment provided under the AWIA or the MHCTSA.

There are a number of concerns with regard to the detail of the implementation of the functions within the ASP, particularly with regard to the impact of implementation on issues such as choice and citizenship. It is within this context that the empirical research, which this chapter draws on, takes place.

Summary of the research

This study aims to identify the evolution of the Adult Support and Protection (Scotland) Act 2007, how the implementation of the legislation has taken place and its impact on service users and carers. This will be undertaken in three distinct stages and this chapter will draw on the emerging findings from stage 1, as described below.

The aim of stage 1 was to track the evolution of the legislation and identify how it developed into its current form from the perspective of a range of key stakeholders through face to face interviews. The interviews included consideration of how theories of citizenship and capacity including rights and responsibilities featured in discussion about the shape of the legislation and what consideration these were given in shaping the final language and intent.

The sample for this stage of the research was identified through discussions with those tasked with implementing the Act and those at Scottish Government who worked on drafting the legislation. The sample included a range of individuals and professionals including medical staff, social work staff and Scottish Government personnel as well as those representing the views of service users and carers.

The interviews were structured around key themes, including concepts of vulnerability considered and appropriate parameters of intervention. This thematic approach aimed to allow for flexibility within the discussions themselves. Furthermore, it acknowledged the different perspectives and motivations of those involved in the development of the legislation and allowed for an exploration of the key themes discussed. It was acknowledged by many that they participated in the development of the legislation almost reluctantly as it was felt that it could be potentially overly restrictive to legislate in this manner. However, interviewees were candid and forthright in their discussion of concerns about perceived overlegislation whilst at the same time protecting the rights of the individuals who may benefit from additional support and/or protection. Much discussion, therefore, took place on the limits of rights and responsibilities, particularly the links between rights and individual autonomy.

Classical theorists such as Paine (1995) contend that individuals had the ability to self-determine prior to the introduction of the state and do not require the state's intervention to uphold self-determination. Others have argued that community relies on individuals to function within defined parameters and, therefore, society has the right to intervene to ensure it can continue to confer rights and provide services to individuals (Faulks, 2000).

It is within this conflict of ideas that the development of the ASP took place. Consequently, those tasked with maintaining order in the lives of individuals such as those within the criminal and civil justice systems had a clearer perspective on the role of the state. Conversely, those within statutory and voluntary welfare systems had greater concerns about the limits of state intervention.

Key themes
Was legislation required?

Overall, it is important to acknowledge that there was a significant measure of consensus on the need for this legislation. Each of the interviewees was able to describe situations where protective legislation would have made the difference between effective support and protection and an inability to intervene. These personal experiences appear to have been crucial in driving the process forward as there was a clear perception amongst some respondents that no other legislative measures could have been used to give protection in the specific situations described. Even where respondents were overall not convinced that legislation was required, they could still cite examples where adults had been unable to be protected, principally because they were unable to find a way through the door to engage the adult or get their permission to provide support. They were further able to acknowledge that without this personal experience they may have felt the legislation was in the words of one respondent 'a sledgehammer to crack a nut'. Examples of cases cited are detailed below.

EXAMPLE 3 – HEALTH STAFF

A patient was being physically abused by his son in his own home and there appeared to be no way in to compel any interventions; getting the patient on their own was problematic and it was clear the son had a great deal of influence and control. Conversely, during our work with this family, the son abused the family dog and via the RSPCA it was significantly easier to get the dog out of the house and to provide protection for it than it was to protect the parents. The key problem with this case was finding a way in to undertake assessment that enabled us to get past the son.

EXAMPLE 4 – SOCIAL WORK STAFF

An adult presents at A&E from a care home with a head inquiry, gets excellent treatment, is well looked after and returns to the care home. At no point is there consideration given to the fact that this may be an adult protection issue depending on how the injury was received. If a child had been admitted with the same injury, more specific and focused enquiries would have been made. This shows lack of engagement of health staff with adult protection and lack of joined-up working in this area.

As previously noted, both the English and Welsh reviews of adult protection frameworks have called for legislation although neither has opted to date to pursue this mechanism. Reasons cited for the need for legislation included the balance of choice and safeguarding, clarity over those to be covered by the legislation and in particular the promotion of inter-agency collaboration (DH, 2009). In addition, the need to promote empowerment to ensure adult protection is not provided at the expense of other qualities of life, including self-determination, was a much-debated issue (see for example O'Keefe et al, 2007). The emerging view from the study described above suggests that this balance was central to the discussions that took place during the evolution of the ASP. The view from the majority of respondents was that, despite the possibility that self-determination might be compromised to some degree in some instances, the option that adults may be left in situations where they were at continuing risk of harm was untenable.

Liberal theories of citizenship suggest this pursuit of private interest, such as behaving in one's private live as one wishes, is crucial in characterising the public–private divide. The civil rights inherent in citizenship protect this divide and, therefore, should protect the private realm, not promote interference or intervention (Faulks, 2000). However, feminists and others have often argued that this view is largely paternalistic and that the public realm more often than not protected the inalienable rights of men rather than all citizens (Lister, 1997). In addition, this private realm can be used further to promote inequality, particularly between the sexes.

Therefore, the emphasis placed on debating the need for this legislation is rooted in traditional liberal theories of citizenship and the right to a private life including self-determination.

User and carer involvement

As described previously, a Steering Group comprising representatives from a wide range of organisations developed the detail of the ASP legislation. They met over a three-year period from 2002 to 2005, serviced by the Scottish Government. Whilst users and carers were not directly involved in this group, a number of consultations on what was then termed the Vulnerable Adults Bill had taken place

prior to the establishment of the group. It was, therefore, felt, particularly by the Scottish Government, that a number of opportunities
had already been created for service users and carers to contribute to
the process of development. However, it was indicated by a number
of members that, although they accepted that an opportunity had
been created via the consultation process for users' and carers' views
to be incorporated, full representation on the steering committee
would have been appropriate. It was clear that those undertaking a
representative role had gone to great lengths to ensure that they did
not, in the words of one respondent, present 'the world according
to me'. There were examples of both virtual and real consultation
groups being established for representatives to discuss the key issues
being raised within the Steering Group.

The development of this legislation in Scotland had the benefit
of the Milan principles, which underpin the MHCTSA, ensuring a
rights-based approach (MacKay, 2011). Consequently, the views of
service users and carers were central to the process of development,
and key safeguards such as advocacy support and clear legal tests were
built into the legislative process. However, it could be argued that,
although key safeguards are present in the ASP legislation, the fact of
being excluded from the Steering Group's detailed deliberations limited the power and control of service users and carers in its final shape.
This is particularly important if you consider the debate about the
concepts considered in driving the need for the legislation described
above. It could be argued that those whose human rights were potentially being compromised were excluded from the decision-making
process to a degree.

Main aim of developing the legislation
There was a general consensus that the main aim of developing the
legislation was to protect a group of adults who, there was significant evidence to suggest, had previously been unable to be protected
through existing processes and procedures. However, whether or not
that perceived gap required legislation was an area of some conten-
tion. There was also an acknowledgement of the impact of high-profile cases such as the Scottish Borders Inquiry (Scottish Executive,
2004b) on adult protection, the demands of politicians following the

inquiry, the Scottish Law Commission report (1997) and, finally, the establishment of key personnel in the Scottish Government to drive adult protection forward.

One of the main drivers for those in this sample appeared to be their own personal work experience and the feelings of helplessness and frustration they felt at being unable to provide effective support and protection to adults at risk of harm. There was further an acknowledgement of the complexities of harm and abuse and the overlapping and flexible nature of these concepts (see, for example, Brown, 2003; Mantell and Scragg, 2008) and that to extract one element of that – self-determination – oversimplified the issue. One respondent noted: 'Without the checks and balances of advocacy, the involvement of the sheriff, etc., this legislation would be a bridge too far.'

There was, however, an underlying perception that if existing legislation had been used appropriately then additional legislation would not have been required. Previous inquiries where social workers and other professionals, particularly health, had not understood the law well enough to apply it appropriately were cited (see for example Stewart, 2008). It was further argued that professionals were more likely to go with codes of practice and guidance rather than thinking about how they might use existing legislation itself imaginatively. Consequently, a view was expressed that existing options should perhaps have been explored more thoroughly before legislation was agreed on. For example support could be provided via Section 47 of the National Assistance Act 1948. This section could be used, for example, to remove an adult from their home if it was thought that it was in the interests of the adult or would prevent injury to the health of the adult. This could have included adults who were aged, infirm of physically incapacitated who were not caring appropriately for themselves or being cared for by others, much like those covered by contemporary adult protection procedures. However, this potential solution was not widely acknowledged or utilised.

In addition, respondents noted that whilst politicians did indeed drive the move towards legislation they were also very concerned about limiting the reach of the state into adults' lives. This was described as: 'They wanted to do what they saw as the right thing but they were also worried about pushing the states boundaries too far.' However, the use of actual case examples and how the legislation might work in practice, provided as evidence during the passage of the legislation, appeared to be significant in making the case to the politicians.

For many, particularly those with a practice background, developing this legislation was viewed as a way to get through the front door. It was noted that the protection orders could be used to create breathing space for service users and professionals to consider the best next move: for example, whether an assessment order or removal order was required and whether or not this might be helpful. It was described by a member of the Steering Group as a way to:

> ...give the service user time to draw breath away from the harmful situation and to say how do you feel about your life, what do you want to do with your days, so that they can stand back and make an informed decision in a non-judgemental environment.

Whilst data on the extent of the population who might benefit from this legislation is sketchy at best (O'Keefe *et al.*, 2007), there is evidence to suggest that, for older people at least, the opportunity to report harm and to be protected from harm is actually welcome (Cooper *et al.*, 2008).

The scope of the legislation

There was a variation in opinion on the scope of the legislation, particularly as this related to the issue of capacity. A split in views occurred over whether or not it was solely meant for those who had capacity or could and should include those who lacked capacity. It appears on the surface to make sense that if the purpose of the legislation was to fill the gap left by the MHCTSA and the AWIA, then it would be used primarily by those who had capacity. One respondent described the aim of the legislation as below:

> This is for those people whom we have all had to walk away from – knowing harm was being perpetrated but being unable to do absolutely anything to help because they didn't lack capacity and were not mentally ill.

This divergence in opinion appeared to depend on what background the respondent came from. Those from learning disability and mental health backgrounds stated clearly that the Act should not be used with those who lacked capacity, as there was already legislation in place to provide protection for those adults. Those respondents with an older people and/or dementia background were clear that the ASP may be used initially to gain access and assess to those adults whose capacity was unclear and that by providing a route for statutory intervention the Act would triage those requiring assessment under other legislative avenues, such as Adults with Incapacity (Scotland) Act 2000. In particular, it was felt that this could be useful in identifying those with an undiagnosed dementia or mental disorder and, consequently, providing care and support: 'Gaining access to hidden dementia sufferers requiring care and support and consequently providing support to their carers could be a real benefit of this legislation.'

The issue of capacity was, therefore, controversial. Those with a practice background within the sample felt that the issue of capacity had been 'fudged' in the legislation, and the code of practice that consequently accompanied the Act had further created confusion about who could or could not be subject to its powers. One respondent noted: 'If you don't have capacity to consent, you don't have capacity to withhold consent.' However, overall there was a view that the Act would focus on providing support and protection to those who had capacity, although it would and should inevitably encompass those whose capacity was unclear and/or who had an undiagnosed mental disorder and hopefully provide a previously unavailable route into ensuring their support needs were met at an earlier stage than would previously have been possible.

These discussions reflect much of the literature in this area with regard to defining capacity and the idea that the lack of competence or capacity reduces the rights of individuals. For example Rawls (1998) notes that there is an underlying assumption that all citizens have the capacity to function as normal members of society. Rawls, therefore, posits a normative construction of society, which is much criticised (see, for example, Beckett, 2006) in that it can be seen to exclude those outwith these parameters, such as those with disabilities. It is interesting, therefore, to note that this conflict of views around capacity, and whether or not the interventions within the ASP should apply to those who lack capacity, could be explained by personal views of a normative society. Of particular consideration may be ascribing individual rights to those who lack capacity.

Vulnerability and risk

Practitioners interviewed particularly focused on the link between vulnerability and the risk of harm. There was further some concern that vulnerability in and of itself was being viewed as equalling limited capacity in terms of requirements for intervention. There was some consideration that there was a lack of clarity, particularly in the code of practice about the thresholds between vulnerability and the risk of harm. One respondent noted that 'lots of people require support but some people actually need protection'. There was a minority view that there was too much of a focus on meeting the three-point legal test rather than on whether or not the adults' vulnerability, in whatever form, required protection. It was posited that an adult could be at risk of harm but not vulnerable and conversely be vulnerable but not at risk of harm. The main questions considered here were: 'Are we talking about protection from harm or are we talking about support for vulnerable people?' and 'Is there a significant difference?' However, it was acknowledged that the legislation does seek to do both. For many, this threshold is important particularly as it means that considerable thought has to go into whether or not a referral is an adult protection referral or a community care referral purely requiring support. The consequences of this lack of clarity were viewed as significant, particularly in terms of information gathering and statistical analysis. In addition, thresholds for significant harm and consequent intervention under the Act were also felt to require clarification.

This link between vulnerability and risk is much discussed (see, for example, Hussein *et al.*, 2007; Cardono, 1999). Whilst they are often discussed, and indeed conceptualised, independently they are also often confused. Cardono (1999), for example, argues that reducing vulnerability actually means reducing risk, particularly as it relates to work in the social sciences, with older people, children or women.

Bornat and Blytheway (2010) further associate the identification of risk factors with the drive towards personalisation and other policies, which impose responsibility on individuals. In addition, they argue that those seen as not managing their lives effectively or perceived as a risk to society are being targeted by overly protective policies. The link between risk and the prevention of future harm has been well made (see, for example, Webb, 2006) and leads to consideration of the role of risk in every day life as a right. However, perceiving risk and vulnerability as inextricably linked means we can all be viewed as vulnerable, passive and dependent at various times in our lives (McLauchlin, 2008). At the same time as demonising the welfare state, social policies have, therefore, been seen to increase its intrusion into the lives of adults (Bornat and Blytheway, 2010). Consequently, this discussion of risk and vulnerability has legitimised the need for the protection from harm of certain groups within society.

Other influencing factors during development

During the evolution of the legislation, respondents were asked to consider what they felt were the other key areas for discussion, which impacted on the final shape. The following summarises the issues identified.

Language and definitions

Use of language and construction of definitions were considered at length. In particular, concepts of vulnerability and abuse formed much of the discussion. One of the main arguments appeared to have focused on replacing the use of the term 'vulnerable'. A particular concern was that the term 'vulnerable adult' places the vulnerability within the adult rather than putting this in context, which includes the adult's interactions with broader society and the circumstances in which they live. Whilst a number of respondents were uncomfortable with the term 'vulnerable', service users and carers indicated a particular distaste for the term for just this reason.

The term 'abuse' was also of some concern, although initially the group used this term. However, the Health Committee of the Scottish Parliament took a different view and were particularly worried about the impact on carers of the use of the term 'abuse'. If, for example, you were a carer at the end of your tether and at risk of harming someone, you would be less likely to seek support if you were to be termed an 'abuser'. However, there was a view amongst a number of respondents that harm was a softer option, which perhaps did not relay the seriousness of a particular situation. One respondent noted in particular that it was a question of degrees: 'I can cause you harm without it being abuse.' There was a perception that the term 'abuse' is closer to criminality than the term 'harm'. Perhaps, because there requires to be an element of assessment about what harm means in terms of the Act, concern was expressed that it may enable grey areas to develop because of the vagaries of professional assessment.

Given the previous discussion about the challenges in defining abuse and the complexity of this changing over time and cultures (Penhale and Parker, 2008), it is to be expected that this issue received much consideration in the evolution of the ASP.

Support and protection
From a service user and carer perspective ensuring that support was as high up the agenda as protection was critical. This involved getting the process and procedures right as there was concern that this could very much depend on the prevailing view in individual teams about how to balance support and protection. The process of assessment, therefore, had to be informed by what outcomes service users themselves wanted. This it was thought would ensure: 'We don't promote a paternalistic attitude; we must be empowering whilst protecting.'

Potential gaps
A number of potential gaps in the legislation were described. Consideration of how the legislation might affect other groups was also thought to be largely unclear and, therefore, a gap – for example:
- asylum seekers;
- addiction and harm caused by addiction;
- links to domestic violence.

One respondent noted that they would have lobbied for a more rigorous legal test in front of the sheriff than what has emerged in the final shape, given the broad range of adults with whom it could potentially be used. There was also a suggestion that the ASP could be used in other settings: for example, protecting prisoners from being bullied. However, it became apparent that, in settings such as prisons, local policies and procedures were felt to be more appropriate, particularly when working within the criminal justice systems. In addition, practitioners cited a period of 'bedding in' for mainstream use before more innovative approaches were considered.

It was proposed that a power approximating a supervision order that allows for ongoing involvement with individual families and that has legal support and an element of compulsion would have been helpful. It was noted that this would recognise that, frequently, you do need the power to work with people longer term rather than the one-off measures that are in place. However, it was not clear how this would have supported the rights-based approach, which underpins the legislation.

Another potential gap was that links to health staff were considered poor and it was hoped that the inter-agency collaboration promoted in the legislation might raise awareness amongst health staff as well as increase the priority afforded to adult protection. A further gap was identified in terms of information sharing: for example, do GPs have to give information about adults if required by other agencies in line with the legislation? There appears to be disagreement over this area: the ASP code of practice states yes they should, but Smith and Patrick (2009) suggest there is no legal obligation for GPs to share information. There are many caveats to the sharing of information and indeed co-operation. Whilst health boards must co-operate with a local authority making enquiries, for example, they can refuse if they do not believe it is consistent with the exercise of its functions. This could also lead to inconsistencies in practice where doctors at A&E do have a duty to report suspected harm to local authority social work departments but GPs do not.

The benefits of good inter-agency collaboration as it relates to adult protection as well as the potential dangers where it is not effective are viewed as a key area for development. There is clear evidence of the outcomes for service users where, for example, information is not shared (see, for example, Scottish Executive, 2004b).

Finally, how do we future-proof this legislation? For example, how are the Royal Colleges incorporating the ASP into their current training, particularly as it relates to responsibilities around referral and multi-disciplinary working, including information sharing? There was an overall view that 'adult protection is where child protection was twenty years ago and that we don't have twenty years to catch up'. However, as the legislation is in its early stages of implementation this view may be somewhat harsh. Social work courses and other inter-disciplinary training courses have increasingly incorporated work on risk and protection with adults in their curriculum. In addition, evaluation and review of the ASP will highlight and propose solutions to some of these key issues: for example, consideration could be given to extending the definition of public bodies to include GPs (Smith and Patrick, 2009).

Fit for purpose

Despite the concerns described above, the majority of respondents felt that the ASP was largely fit for purpose. In addition, there was a sense that it was becoming triage legislation for assessment following which adults were often being offered support or protective measures under other parts of the pyramid of protective legislation in Scotland: for example, the MHCTSA or the AWIA. The hope was this ensured that those perhaps previously hidden were being offered appropriate support.

Despite concerns about the evidencing of undue pressure as highlighted previously, there was a view that without this the rest of the powers would, in effect, be toothless. However, for the NHS, it is noted that this continues to be a difficult area, given that they do not treat patients without their consent.

A further ongoing challenge is to measure whether or not the ASP has made a difference to the lives of individuals in order that evidence can be gathered on whether or not this approach is meeting its aims. There is at the moment a focus on numbers rather than on outcomes for individuals. This leaves a crucial gap in what we know to date about how the legislation is working in practice. However, research was commissioned by the Scottish Government in mid 2011 to examine outcomes for individuals in detail.

Conclusion

Whilst views have been expressed that this legislation could be seen as draconian, there have clearly been many situations where professionals have been unable to protect adults at risk of harm. This experience by many of the representatives involved in the evolution of the ASP drove forward the development and detail of this legislation. There was, furthermore, a general view that adults had been protected that would otherwise not have been assisted through the use of the ASP to date, although this is anecdotal at best.

There was some concern expressed that it would not be viable in the current financial climate to continue with two protection systems – one for children and one for adults – but that in the future we would be likely to see a public protection system for all citizens. However, this does appear to fly in the face of the assertion in Scotland that the protective agenda focuses on service user/patients' rights rather than public protection. Therefore, consideration of the basis of any joint system would require focusing on the principles established in current protective legislation.

There was also concern that we as society have to accept that there are limits to intervention:

> What if someone refuses consent and you cannot show evidence of undue pressure or indeed there has been none? As there are no other options in terms of statutory intervention, we may have to accept this limitation to protect adults' right to self-determination.

One final consideration may be where people do not see themselves as vulnerable or at risk of harm and, consequently, will not seek out support. This very much links to the notion that vulnerability is viewed as something inherent in the individual rather than being a product of the context within which the adult is living. If adults do not view themselves within this framework when appropriate, then more people will slip through the safety net. Awareness-raising of the supportive aspects of this and other legislation may be helpful.

This chapter has considered the links between risk, vulnerability, capacity and citizenship as they relate to adult protection within the context of the evolution of the ASP in Scotland. The key discussions

that informed the basis of the ASP reflect the conflicts over definitions of capacity, constructs of normative societies and the rights and
responsibilities of contemporary citizenship. It is gratifying that such
serious consideration was given to this increased intervention in the
lives of adults.

CHAPTER 4

Citizenship and Capacity – An Exploration of the Links with Adult Protection

Introduction

This chapter will consider the concept of citizenship and its links to capacity within an exploration of Section 35 of the Adult Support and Protection (Scotland) Act 2007. The central argument within this chapter is that those individuals unable to perform the expected functions of citizens or who are, for whatever reason, structurally excluded from claiming their rights as citizens are likely to be treated inequitably. In addition, there is consequently the potential for them to be subject to state intervention regardless of their ability to make their own decisions (to have capacity or not). Essentially, the following is an exploration of the notion of being a citizen and acting as a citizen (Lister, 1998) and the impact on those who are unable to act as a citizen for whatever reason despite legally being one.

Concepts and theories of citizenship stretch back to the ancient Greeks in the fourth and fifth centuries and are generally modelled on a notion of the relationship between the individual and the society in which they live (Beckett, 2006). Those whose citizenship is curtailed, compromised or made fragile by their lack of ability in certain areas, due to unemployment or a disability, are often consequently not viewed as citizens. This effectively illustrates the potential for citizenship to be conditional.

The United Nations Convention on the Rights of Persons with Disabilities (UN, 2006), ratified by the UK government in June 2009, marked a significant shift in approaches to people with disabilities, whatever they might be: for example, learning disability, physical disability or mental disorder. It consolidates decades of work by the disability movement to have people with disabilities viewed as active members of society rather than as objects to be protected and treated regardless of their own views. It is further, perhaps, a useful illustration of the move towards the attribution of full citizenship rights as a goal to which all members of society should aspire and indeed expect. A further question might be to consider the parameters of these rights and to whom they might be applied. Does this, for example, include those who lack capacity or those who for other structural reasons are generally excluded from society by, for example, class, gender and/or race?

Concepts of citizenship

What do we mean by citizenship in the twenty-first century? How do we define citizenship? What influences our thinking and does this change over time and across cultures? Marshall (1950) is perhaps regarded as the originator of modern welfare approaches to citizenship. He suggests that, in general, there are three levels of citizenship rights: civil, political and social (see Table 4.1).

Table 4.1: Three levels of citizenship (Marshall, 1950).

Civil	Protects legal rights such as privacy and the right to a fair trial
Political	Allows for participation in the decision-making process of the country: for example, the right to vote
Social	The state's collective responsibility for the welfare of all citizens

Marshall (1950), consequently, envisages that social and welfare services, as representatives of the state, would be integral to ensuring that the social rights of citizenship were delivered, particularly to those who required support.

Contemporary liberal and pluralist approaches to citizenship consider all of the above elements as important but differ in their assessment of whether or not these rights are likely to be available to everyone in society (Beckett, 2006). Kymlicka and Young (see, for example, Kymlicka, 1995; Young, 1990) argue over how to ensure that marginalised or sub-groups within society can claim their basic citizenship rights. They both acknowledge that these groups demand special rights to facilitate their broader participation in society: for example, the modification of organisations to allow members to wear turbans or veils; or the creation of special circumstances such as affirmative action in the US to create equality of access across all its citizens and to balance the workforce. Whilst Young (1990, cited in Faulks, 2000) essentially rejects liberalist notions of the universalist concept of citizenship (all citizens are the same and have access to the same set of rights) as denying the diversity within society, Kymlicka (1995) asserts that group rights, including those marginalised by existing societal structures, can in fact be accommodated within a liberalist/universalist framework.

There are, therefore, a significant number of definitions and concepts of citizenship that continue to cause debate. Nevertheless, there is a common thread, generally perceived to be the balancing of rights and responsibilities (Lawson, 2001). The context of those rights and responsibilities varies throughout the various concepts, as does the balancing of those elements, often thought to be a conditional relationship (Beckett, 2006). Further, the prevalent concept of citizenship in any society is likely to be linked to the political systems and, to a lesser degree, the ideology of the political party in power (MacKay, 2011): for example, in the UK, citizenship is thought to have emerged from individual liberalism, which takes a rights-based approach. This argues that the focus of the political system should be to protect the civil, political and social rights of the individual in line with Marshall's (1950) model.

This concept has been criticised by many including Lister, who argues that this is an 'impoverished version of citizenship' (Lister, 1997, p. 23), which reduces individuals to a passive role that enables them to retreat into their own privacy, meeting their own needs without contributing to the broader community and/or society.

In addition, the changing nature of the world into a global market has led to the consideration of both national and global citizenship (human rights) as different and perhaps competing concepts. Lynch (1992), for example, considers that there are levels of citizenship, which are focused on ethnic, national and international considerations, whilst Cogan and Derricott (2000) suggest a concept of multi-dimensional citizenship with four parts: personal, social, temporal and spatial.

A common thread in these arguments, however, is a view that citizenship is an evolving concept, the discussion of which has driven forward the conversion of needs into rights. It has further been argued (Barnes and Bowl, 2001) that concepts of citizenship provide a useful way of understanding how those with characteristics that set them apart from mainstream society – for example, mental health problems or disabilities – are excluded from society.

In the UK, the prevailing concept of citizenship has varied, often according to the political ideology of the government of the moment. MacKay (2011), for example, argues that the last Conservative government considered a narrow view of citizenship that excluded many disadvantaged groups within society, creating an individualised model of citizenship that focused on traditional Conservative values including the rolling back of the state with significant levels of individual responsibility being viewed as the norm. Citizenship was, therefore, essentially conditional on meeting individual responsibilities as a citizen: for example, employment and appropriate social behaviour. Dwyer (2004), however, argues that this model of citizenship created negative civil and legal rights and weakened positive social rights. New Labour, from 1997, attempted to distance itself from this model of citizenship, considering mutual responsibility to be more appropriate and taking a more positive approach to civil, legal and social rights. They still, however, attached conditions to citizenship rights. These included a limiting of social rights, particularly where individualised behaviour could be deemed harmful or inappropriate, and this has, it could be argued, consequently allowed for a greater level of state intervention in adults' lives where these conditions were not met.

Citizenship has further been defined as a process of proactive engagement in a radical democracy, the aim of this engagement being the achievement of human rights for all citizens and these rights being determined on the basis of a universal acceptance of vulnerability (Beckett, 2006). This model, as Beckett (2006) points out, avoids marking out groups as other and in so doing makes it clear that we are all vulnerable in terms of disability, racism, sexism, poverty or other forms of social exclusion including isolation. This links clearly to the study by O'Keefe *et al* (2007), which indicates that isolation and loneliness are key indicators of those who experience abuse. Beckett (2006) further argues that an analysis of contemporary social movements must go hand in hand with the development of new models of citizenship. However, this notion of universal vulnerability is not one which can be embraced easily, as many people do not wish to consider that they may be vulnerable at some point in their lives and, consequently, that their citizenship and the rights associated with this may be compromised.

Therefore, when we consider fulfilling our citizenship obligations and achieving the rights associated with this concept, we consider the type of responsibilities we may have to fulfil: for example, economic contributions to society through employment, parenting and the production of a new workforce as well as, perhaps, the creative and artistic endeavour in developing the societies we live in. What, therefore, of those who live outwith that paradigm of citizenship? What does it mean for them and what are the implications for their lives? There is an underlying assumption that citizenship and aspiring to be a good citizen (however that is being defined) are positive attributes and that those living outwith this framework are somehow construed as in deficit. This then potentially means that those perceived to be outwith the citizenship paradigm have fewer rights and so perhaps could be made subject to interventions that the majority of society would find unacceptable.

Capacity and adult protection

Defining and assessing capacity is a complex legal and medical issue outwith the scope of this volume. Yet having capacity to make decisions about your own life as an adult is often the difference between being subject to state-sponsored intervention or not. The Adults with Incapacity (Scotland) Act 2000 and the Mental Health Capacity Act 2005 in England and Wales define the parameters of capacity and provide for powers of intervention deemed as supporting adults who lack capacity and their families to make decisions about their day-to-day lives both in a welfare and financial context. Therefore, clear provisions have been made to support individuals who cannot for whatever reason make decisions for themselves where they have been assessed as not having capacity, either through an acquired cognitive or genetic impairment. The power to make those decisions is passed on to someone else who will, in theory, have their best interests at heart and who will make decisions that they know the individuals would want. Perhaps it could be argued they are being supported to claim their rights as citizens. However, could it also mean they are no longer citizens without rights to make their own decisions and to contribute more generally to a broader society? Lister (1998) argues that just because they do not act as citizens does not mean they are no longer citizens.

Therefore, put crudely, society has argued that those without capacity have diminished citizenship rights that are then given to others to obtain for them on their behalf – this may include family members or indeed staff of statutory organisations such as social work or social services. However, the legislation at the heart of this volume, the ASP, also provides for powers of intervention (overriding consent with evidence of undue pressure) in adult's lives where they have capacity. How do we reconcile this with the concept of citizenship described above? How are we able to compromise those rights by intervening in the lives of adults who have capacity to make decisions about their own life and any support they may require? Is it appropriate, therefore, to argue that those individuals who are unable to meet the conditions defined within the prevailing model of citizenship are more likely to be subject to state intervention in how they live their lives that those who are not – regardless of capacity? The following considers this in more detail as it links to adult protection.

One way of compromising an individual's citizenship rights is to consider that they are vulnerable by way of outside pressure to live their life in a particular way: for example, to allow particular practices, such as theft, physical and sexual violence; or to require that they exhibit behaviour that is viewed as contrary to the norm, such as anti-social behaviour. Consequently, the underlying concept is that regardless of the fact that they have capacity to make decisions for themselves, their ability to use that capacity effectively is compromised either by outside pressure or some other context or form of activity that renders them vulnerable.

Consider the above within the Scottish legislation of the ASP. None of the powers should be utilised without the consent of the adult, and indeed this is the case in other jurisdictions' policy frameworks. However, the ASP does allow for overriding the consent of the adult, despite having capacity, with the agreement of a sheriff, if there appears to be undue pressure being applied to the adult to withhold their consent by external sources, such as by the perpetrator of the harm. The issue of undue pressure and the necessary evidence to prove undue pressure (the sheriff must hold a reasonable belief that the adult is being prevented from giving their consent) (Calder, 2010) is a contentious one. Smith and Patrick (2009) argue that any adult being subject to an order granted over their consent may be able to point out that their right to a private life has been infringed and, depending on how the order was exercised, that this potentially constitutes an unlawful deprivation of liberty under Article 5 of the ECHR.

To illustrate this more effectively, consider the example below.

EXAMPLE 5

Andrew, who has learning disabilities, mobility problems and a severe hearing impairment, was admitted to hospital having sustained a head injury. His home carer found him unconscious and called an ambulance. Over the past nine months, Andrew has had numerous admissions with falls, fractures and unexplained major bruising. Andrew says he has become clumsy lately, but no physical cause has been found. Health, social care and housing services have been involved with Andrew over a number of years. At present, his support includes domestic help, housing support, meals on wheels and a treatment involving a district nurse. After being discharged, as the nurse was changing a dressing, Andrew disclosed to her that his son had actually caused the injury as well as the previous injuries. He went on to say his son had a drugs problem and became physically violent towards him on pension days, when he refused to give him more money. He insisted the nurse keep this information confidential as he did not wish his son to get into trouble.

The above example illustrates where an individual chooses to prioritise his relationship with his son over the fact that he is being both financially and physically abused by him. Consequently, it is assumed that some outside pressure is compromising their ability to make acceptable decisions about how they live their life.

How do we delineate then between the above example and one where an adult makes a decision to continue to drink or eat too much even though it is damaging their health with a subsequent impact on society, such as health costs, and perhaps their behaviour is impacting on their day-to-day relationships both in a work and family environment. Would the state consider intervention in both these sets of circumstances? It seems unlikely, although this may be dependent on other factors including whether or not the behaviours impacted on society through criminal behaviour. Therefore, it appears as though it is the context within which these behaviours take place that ultimately defines whether or not interventions take place in the private lives of individuals. Do they have capacity? Are they subject to external pressure or harm of some kind? Are their behaviours visible to broader society? They are, for example, more likely to be visible to broader society if welfare services are involved either as a result of unacceptable behaviour or their broader circumstances.

It may be that it is a combination of the above factors that ultimately leads to intervention by the state in the private lives of adults, even those who have capacity to make their own decisions.

Citizenship and adult protection

Politicians often use the term 'citizen' to outline the responsibilities of their populations in a framework of equality: for example, good citizens may be viewed as producing social capital through employment, social networks and other more general contributions to broader society. The state provides care and protection when required but in return you are responsible for living a good life as a citizen, in effect being a citizen. Tony Blair stated in 1996 that 'a modern notion of citizenship gives rights but demands obligations, shows respect but wants it back, grants opportunity but insists on responsibility' (Blair, 1996, p. 218). More recently, Prime Minister David Cameron's Big Society concept posits a view that society must take care of its own and that individual citizens should, in fact, be shoring up the rolling back of the state by making contributions through effectively providing elements of what have traditionally been public services. This underpinning principle of how we in contemporary Britain should operate reflects a concept of citizenship that values responsibility as a core consideration. However, it should be acknowledged that the concept of Big Society is not considered mainstream within a Scottish context and with the election in spring 2011 of the Scottish National Party to the first majority government in the devolved Scottish Parliament it is unlikely to gain much traction in the near future.

It is clear from existing research, academic literature and current political thinking in the UK that there are a range of models and concepts of citizenship under consideration. However, for the purposes of debate about adult protection we may consider as a broad theme the impact of a conditional approach to citizenship, described above, which has been most in favour in the UK in recent times.

It could be argued that attaching conditions to citizenship immediately ensures exclusion from these rights for certain groups unable to meet the terms. The rest of this chapter explores whether or not any of the groups so affected are likely to be subject to adult protection procedures such as those considered under the ASP as described in Chapter 3 and other policy interventions discussed in this volume. Finally, consideration will be given as to whether their exclusion from citizenship rights is likely to create an artificial boundary from which they are unable to escape.

To what extent, therefore, do we consider the parameters of state intervention into the lives of citizens and how much of this is condoned or justified by the underlying assumptions or constructs about what constitutes citizenship in the UK in the twenty-first century? Within any citizenship model there are legal rights, but it is not just what the law says but also what it implies: for example, its procedural rights; how the law is upheld on information, relationships, decision-making, representation and social rights; and how the above promote wider life chances and quality of life. Harris (1999), for example, argues that procedural rights are more easily claimable for those on the margins of citizenship. However, some people will require support to claim even these rights, and this is where welfare services and staff need to support individuals.

Those people who are unable to claim, or require support to claim their citizenship rights – who might perhaps be categorised as being citizens rather than acting as citizens (Lister, 1998) – are more likely to be in receipt of services and so to have compulsory intervention in their lives.

Those adults defined as being at risk of harm under the act are:

Section 3 (1)

(a) are unable to safeguard their own well-being, property, rights or other interests;

(b) are at risk of harm; and

(c) because they are affected by disability, mental disorder, illness of physical or mental infirmity, are more vulnerable to being harmed than adults who are not so affected.

And

Section 3 (2)

An adult is at risk of harm for the purposes of subsection (1) if another person's conduct is causing (or is likely to cause) the adult to be harmed or the adult is engaging (or is likely to engage) in conduct which causes (or is likely to cause) self-harm (ASP, 2007).

The question at the core of the argument under consideration within this chapter is whether those likely to be subject to the powers of the ASP and other adult protection measures are those who would be categorised as being citizens rather than those acting as citizens. In addition, it is perhaps helpful also to consider what aspects of their role as citizens might make them more likely to be subject to statutory intervention.

When you examine the framework for the ASP above, and consider the key triggers for intervention, these are likely to be an aspect of context or behaviour, which reflect vulnerability, but does this necessarily mean that your citizenship rights are made more fragile? This might perhaps be the case where the situation can be linked to an overriding of your consent to intervention, regardless of your capacity to make those decisions as within the ASP (Section 35).

Perhaps, therefore, it can be argued that those individuals who are citizens but who fail to act as citizens are more likely to be subject to statutory interventions to protect themselves. However, the question remains – is it their limited or fragile citizenship that makes intervention more likely or is it their overall vulnerability, which makes their citizenship fragile and so compromises their social rights as citizens?

What then is the difference between how we view the individuals who are more likely to be subject to statutory intervention than those who are not? It appears from the above that it is the context within which an individual's 'vulnerability' or risk of harm is considered – essentially, their ability to claim their citizenship rights for themselves, such as to be safe and protected, which appears to make the difference. The level of exposure of their risk of harm also contributes to the likelihood of intervention, consensual or not.

The following model is presented to illustrate the potential pathways for care and support for those acting as a citizen and simply being a citizen.

Acting as a citizen:
- decision made to indulge in behaviour that puts the citizen at risk whether by him/herself or from an external source;
- no state intervention unless the citizen actively seeks it out for him/herself;
- exception – where harmful behaviour is brought to attention of authorities by others, such as through criminal behaviour.

Being a citizen:
- decision made to indulge in behaviour which puts the citizen at risk either by him/herself or from an external source;
- state intervention **can be** imposed via policy, procedure and/or legislation, such as banning order, removal order;
- exception – where undue pressure cannot be shown.

There may be additional aspects to this model, including gender, class and ethnicity.

Therefore, those individuals who are citizens in a legal sense but who fail to act as citizens are more likely to be subject to statutory interventions to protect themselves. However, the question remains – is it their limited or fragile citizenship that makes intervention more likely or is it their overall vulnerability or risk of harm, which makes their citizenship fragile and so compromises their social rights as citizens?

One further area of consideration is whether or not we are now replacing consideration of citizenship with that of human rights to allow for a global rather than national perspective. On a positive note, this would seem to allow for the development of a level playing field: for example, regardless of the gross domestic product of a country its citizens are considered to be subject to human rights legislation on a global level. Does this discussion of human rights for all negate the need for a discussion of citizenship at a local level?

Conclusion

Concepts of citizenship, both ancient and modern, appear, consciously or not, to have had a clear impact on how policy and legislation in the protection of adults at risk of harm have developed, particularly as this links to the ASP. The limits to citizenship for those unable to meet the conditions and the rights of individuals to be protected appear to be connected in a structural and, it could be argued, potentially oppressive manner. The consequences of this link seem to be increased intrusion by the state into the lives of those considered to be at the margins of citizenship. Clearly, concepts of vulnerability and capacity are joined to a degree, although the parameters of this are not clear.

Society must question whether this is acceptable, and if not then how is this limit to citizenship and the potential for consequent state-sponsored intrusion to be achieved whilst providing protection where it is required. Perhaps as the legislation develops in Scotland and the impact of policy is evaluated in other parts of the UK a clearer picture will emerge of the impact on the lives of those at risk of harm, and preventative work will be able to be employed to both support and protect adults to achieve their own outcomes.

CHAPTER 5

Emerging Challenges in the Implementation of the Adult Support and Protection (Scotland) Act 2007

Introduction

This chapter will draw on aspects of the empirical research described in Chapter 3 to identify and discuss the emerging challenges in the implementation of this legislation. An examination of how the new statutory powers have been used will be undertaken in the context of the operation of the newly formed multi-agency adult protection committees. Finally, consideration will be given as to how these emerging themes link to the concepts of citizenship and capacity described earlier in the volume as well as to recent research on adult protection carried out in Scotland prior to implementation of the ASP (Hogg *et al.*, 2009a).

An electronic survey of adult protection leads in local authorities was carried out as Stage 2 of a study that aims to identify the evolution of the Adult Support and Protection (Scotland) Act 2007, how the implementation of the legislation has taken place and its impact on service users and carers. The project is being undertaken in three distinct stages and this chapter will draw on the relevant elements of the emerging findings from stage 2. Stage 1 of the study examined the evolution of the legislation and included interviews with key stakeholders in the design and content of the Act; this material will also be drawn on where appropriate. In addition to the above, a sample of the biennial reports produced by Adult Protection Committees in 2010 was analysed to further establish key themes and corroborate those identified via the other sources.

Framework

Hogg *et al.* (2009a) undertook a detailed study of inter-agency collaboration in adult support and protection between 2005 and 2007, before the ASP was passed or implemented. Whilst the focus of the study was specifically on inter-agency collaboration, it also provides a useful baseline on how the support and protection of adults at risk of harm were being undertaken in Scotland at that time. This gives a helpful framework within which to consider the early implementation of the ASP. The Hogg *et al.* (2009a) study examined more than forty adult protection cases with a range of key features including multiple experiences of abuse. In addition, the cases researched related to a wide range of disabilities and conditions:

> including older people with and without dementia or neurological conditions, and people with intellectual disabilities, as well as individuals with brain damage, mental health problems and difficulties in mediating their social relationships. (Hogg *et al.*, 2009a, p. 6)

Good practice was found across all the key agencies involved, including social work, health and the police. However, considerable challenges were also identified, which meant that the support and protection of adults at risk of harm often fell short of what was required to care for them effectively.

Hogg *et al.* (2009a) establish that much of the work being undertaken under the auspices of adult support and protection was extremely complex. This was found to be the case both within the context in which the harm was taking place (particularly interpersonal relationships) and within the inter-agency collaboration required to address the harm and protect the adult. In addition, Hogg *et al.* (2009a) realised that the legal framework for intervention was complex and involved detailed inter-agency collaboration, with social workers at the centre. A significant feature of this inter-agency collaboration appeared to be a lack of understanding about each other's roles, expectations not being met and the creation of much confusion and frustration, which prevented agency processes working appropriately.

Findings from the above study were grouped into themes:

- occupational cultures;
- how cases were conceptualised;
- operational considerations (reporting abuse, investigating allegations of abuse, review and case conferences, inter-agency collaboration, risk assessment, legal considerations, independent advocacy, reflective learning);
- adults at risk, their families and perpetrators (alleged victims and victims of abuse, family members, alleged perpetrators and perpetrators of abuse).

The Hogg *et al.* (2009a) study further found that the issues which impact on adult protection are inter-related and on three main levels: the wider cultural context which informs the way in which agencies work; the processes which shape how a given case is conceptualised as a formal adult protection case or otherwise; and the contingent procedural or operational actions through which the professionals engage and deal with the case (Hogg *et al.*, 2009a, p. 67). The following key themes will make links to the relevant aspects of the author's research alongside the links to citizenship and capacity.

How has the ASP been used?

During the first two years of its implementation (2008–10), information informally collected by lead adult protection officers (DeSouza, 2011) indicates that:

- thirty-eight protection orders were granted (nineteen with the power of arrest attached);
- four removal orders were granted (one applied for and not granted);
- no assessment orders were granted (one applied for and not granted).

Perhaps more interestingly, almost 40% of local authorities in Scotland had not used any protection orders at all. However, this is perhaps to be expected given that of the 78% of referrals received under the auspices of the ASP legislation that reached Inquiry stage during this period, only 20% became full investigations. Furthermore, just over 1% of all referrals ended with protection orders being considered (DeSouza, 2011). In addition, it appears as though many referrals dealt with initially through the ASP ultimately ended up being channelled through other legislative avenues, such as the Adults with Incapacity (Scotland) Act 2000. Consequently, it could be argued that the ASP could be construed as triage legislation, used to identify the most appropriate routes to support and protection, often through voluntary means or through other legislative measures, rather than as formal use of the ASP protective measures themselves.

In addition to the above findings, the significant increase in the number of referrals received (principally from the police) since the introduction of the ASP has had considerable resource implications for local authorities (DeSouza, 2011). However, this does suggest that for the most part adults may have been able to be protected without the need to invoke the legislative powers enshrined within the ASP. What then, it could be argued, is the purpose of the legislation? A view is emerging that protection orders are being used as a last resort and as a means of gaining the co-operation of adults and their families, primarily on a voluntary basis. It has been suggested by respondents that the existence of the protection orders means they do not require to be used. Therefore, practitioners have expressed a view that without the legislation they may not be able to gain access to adults at risk of harm. Despite the fact that the legislative protective measures have been used in a small number of cases only, the general perception is that they are still required to gain the co-operation of both service users and potential perpetrators in order to reduce the risk of existing and future harm and to provide support and protection.

This corresponds to the views of practitioners and others during the evolution of the legislation – that they needed a way 'to get in the front door'. The ASP appears to have provided that opportunity. However, it is also clear from the above that for the majority of adults voluntary engagement has been achieved where required for the purposes of support and protection. Whilst DeSouza (2011) details information gathered informally from across local authorities in Scotland, it is based on a survey carried out by Convention of Scottish Local Authorities (COSLA), which is unpublished. However, there are clear challenges in gathering consistent data on the use of the ASP and this is explored in more detail later in this chapter.

Main challenges in implementation and issues for future development

The following key themes were identified using the sources described above. It is interesting to note that they can all be linked to the three levels that Hogg *et al.* (2009a) identify as being of interest from their study. Contextual issues such as organisational culture, the conceptualisation of what constitutes adult protection and the associated processes including thresholds all feature in a consideration of the operation of the ASP to date, as do operational issues such as referral processes and inter-agency collaboration.

Definitions/Processes

Despite the guidance accompanying the ASP legislation, there continues to be confusion over what adult protection actually is and how an adult at risk of harm is defined in practice. The process of managing this has been seen to get in the way of support being provided. A clearer definition of an adult at risk, as well as simpler guidance regarding use of the Act in relation to adults who lack capacity, were felt to be required. There appear, therefore, to be persistent challenges in conceptualising just what an adult protection case looks like. This is further linked to the notion of thresholds, particularly with regard to what constitutes an inquiry under the ASP, when this becomes an investigation and how this is recorded. This is particularly important when considering whether or not a referral is recorded as adult protection or not, and the impact of this decision both in resource terms and for evidence of effectiveness or not of the legislation itself.

Care vs. control

Consideration of issues of capacity and choice, particularly the adult's right to self-determination, continue to challenge professionals implementing the legislation in practice. Capacity and self-determination arguments – for example, the right to choose to live in a particular way (discussed in more detail in Chapter 3) – are playing out in practice, and it appears that professional judgement is being used to resolve this debate. In addition, there appear to be different approaches to this issue dependent on the operational culture within which the practitioner functions. This may be linked to the classic 'Berlin wall' between the medical and social model of care (see, for example, Glasby, 2003) including conflicting constructs of health and social care needs and how these should be met. Traditionally, health care is provided to patients, whilst social care aims to empower service users in meeting their own needs. However, it is unclear to what extent this link can be made without a detailed case analysis.

Capacity

According to an ASP Lead Officer, there is a view that sheriffs are inconsistent in granting protection orders where there is uncertainty over an adult's capacity:

> One sheriff will not grant an order if the adult does not understand because of a lack of capacity. I have sympathy with this view as the Act is based on the adult consenting to inquiries being made, an investigation being carried out, medical examination etc. If you don't know if they have capacity to grant consent it's not possible to grant the order.

There appears, therefore, to be a lack of clarity as to whether or not an order can be granted where an adult lacks capacity or their capacity is uncertain. Keenan (2011) acknowledges that whilst there is no statutory provision inbuilt, the code of practice associated with the act was amended to allow for adults with incapacity to go before a sheriff (Scottish Government, 2009). There may also be issues here with regard to the amount of time it takes to obtain an order under AWIA, which would appear to be the most appropriate route for the protection of someone who lacks capacity. Protection orders under the ASP were viewed by respondents as much quicker to obtain.

Respondents appear to indicate that if an adult cannot give their consent for an application for a protection order, owing to lack of capacity, a local authority would require to provide evidence of undue pressure for a sheriff to consider granting the order. However, if the ASP is intended to identify those currently not protected, this group is likely to include those who lack capacity.

It is, perhaps, helpful to consider the conflict of opinion with regard to whether or not the ASP was meant to support and protect those who lacked capacity, as discussed earlier in this volume. This conflict of opinion may have inadvertently led to a lack of clarity over this issue within the guidance and indeed the legislation itself.

Recording/Sharing information

It has been apparent that there is a lack of consistency in the recording of data with regard to the ASP in Scotland (Scottish Government, 2010). Consistency in recording information is viewed as important to identify key gaps and in particular how ASP protection orders are addressing the needs of those at risk of harm. A more fundamental problem is that of thresholds; whether or not a referral is recorded as an ASP referral can be very much dependent on professional judgement. This study found that a combination of meeting the legal three-point test, professional judgement and a complex interaction of issues such as extent of harm, impact of harm, level of risk and future risk was used to classify adult protection enquiries. The Hogg *et al.* (2009b) study recommend that a consistent approach to risk assessment with specific reference to determining thresholds was required to achieve consistency and convergence of judgements on the threshold for adult protection intervention. It would appear this work still requires to be further developed in practice.

There is a further impact on this lack of consistency in applying criteria for conceptualising an adult protection case. The variation of approach suggests that gathering information that is consistent is complex and often problematic. Furthermore, the impact of the concordat on the relationship between the Scottish Government and the local authorities in Scotland limits the power of the Scottish Government to demand that data is collected in a routine manner. Consequently, this has meant that there is no consistent core data set across Scotland (Scottish Government, 2010) and, therefore, reports submitted, for example the biennial reports, may provide an inconsistent and uneven picture of development of systems and implementation of procedures. Reports from Adult Protection Committees (APCs) should be standardised to give a comparable picture across the country. In analysing a small sample of the biennial reports it is clear that different structures were used and different emphasis placed across the local authorities. However, there is general consistency in the key themes covered, principally: training, awareness-raising, ASP activity and critical case reviews.

Parameters of the legislation

It appears that, as would be expected, the main focus of work in the first two years of the ASP has been around what could perhaps be termed 'mainstream' issues of harm such as self-harm and physical, primarily with older people, people with learning disabilities and those with mental health problems. However, the ASP also seems to have been utilised to support women who have experienced domestic violence and others. This may be an area for further development in the future and could include those who self-harm, although this is a complex and controversial area for intervention. How far does the legislation stretch in its aim to cover all settings? To what extent should it be used in care homes where regulatory bodies should be picking up issues? Should it extend to prisoners being bullied in prison? Should it be used in hospital wards? The potential overlaps with other legislative avenues are significant and there is likely to be considerable links required to both criminal legislation and criminal justice teams. The author's research revealed that these areas were still being explored and tested out by practitioners.

Inter-agency collaboration

A key driver of the ASP was to promote good inter-agency collaboration with a duty to collaborate placed on a range of agencies. However, whilst all APCs appear to include health and social workers as well as the police, there is significant variation in the extent to which other agencies are involved, such as education and the Care Commission as well as users and carers. In addition, the work of the APCs appears to vary, although in general it is focused around monitoring, awareness-raising and training.

There have been particular challenges in working with GPs and indeed with health services more broadly. Concern has been expressed that health staff do not 'own the agenda' and consequently have not prioritised it appropriately. As the local authority had the primary responsibility for implementing the ASP legislation, a view was expressed that it was principally their responsibility and consequently of their staff, despite the requirement that it be done in partnership. Hogg *et al.* (2009a, 2009b) identify concerns with the engagement of health. This appeared to be linked to the narrowness of the definition of health (Penhale *et al.*, 2007), given its multi-faceted organisational structure: for example, good engagement of GPs and Community Psychiatric Nurses (CPNs) was found in adult protection in some areas, principally where there was a history of good collaboration. However, the author's research described above found significant concerns about the engagement of GPs in the adult protection process, particularly with regard to the sharing of information. In addition, there was concern that agencies such as the Department for Work and Pensions (DWP) were not compelled to share information. One respondent cited serious concerns about the level of buy-in from health colleagues, in particular those key settings such as accident and emergency where initial referrals might be made. Referral information contained in biennial reports indicates that referrals from this setting are limited, indeed often almost non-existent (see, for example, Adult Protection Renfrewshire, 2010). However, given the vagaries of the recording system it is difficult to be definite. Whilst it was acknowledged that health staff would recognise the issues, there was a view expressed that they may not follow this through and that it would not be seen as their duty. Indeed, North Lanarkshire Adult Protection Committee (2010) in their first biennial report note that the number of referrals from the NHS is low, ranging from zero to five across the months considered. It should be noted that Hogg *et al.* (2009b) recommend that a core set of staff with an adult protection responsibility be developed within the NHS with the capacity to work with the lead local authority officer in a flexible integrated way. It is unclear to what extent this crucial link has been made.

However, there have been positive developments across agency boundaries including, for example, the development of a west of Scotland protocol for responding to adults at risk of harm, which is similar to that for child protection. This protocol aims to provide consistency for adults in the west of Scotland should protective measures be required (South Lanarkshire Council, 2010).

Finally, the independent nature of the chair of APCs has, according to a significant number of respondents, been viewed positively as an objective voice. It was felt that the chair had been able to challenge all agencies, creating a sense of equity, despite the fact that the local authority has the lead role. However, there have also been less positive views of the role of independent chair, particularly with regard to how they view their role: for example, as leading ASP without an operational structure; or having an objective eye on the progress of work. Essentially, concern was expressed that, whilst having a clear view on leading the work of ASP in their localities, chairs were often too distant from operational frameworks to be able to direct the work at this level and clarity was required over the parameters of this role. Ensuring all the key stakeholder agencies are implementing the legislation appropriately remains an area for development.

Public awareness

Public awareness of adult protection is still felt to be underdeveloped, despite awareness-raising campaigns at both a national and local level. This may be linked to concepts of vulnerability and the concern that many adults do not see themselves as likely to be at risk of harm (Beckett, 2006). In addition, there is a public perception that this issue is primarily a concern for older people. Making sure everyone knows about the powers in the Act and perhaps more importantly to whom it might apply are key tasks for APCs and units within local authorities to ensure that adults do not fall through the net. Mechanisms such as radio and press campaigns have been utilised to localise the national campaign developed by the Scottish Government. The Hogg et al. (2009b) study indicates that awareness-raising should be within the remit of APCs and adult protection units.

It is unclear from the first biennial reports produced by APCs in 2010 to what extent awareness-raising amongst the public has taken place and indeed what impact this may have had, although there are, of course, challenges in attributing success to particular mechanisms. However, what is clear is that referrals increased sharply across Scotland following implementation of the ASP: for example, in Renfrewshire in the first full year of implementation (2009/10) there were 611 referrals and in the previous six months there had been 124 (Adult Protection Renfrewshire, 2010). However, the vast majority of these referrals came from the police, not the public, and ultimately of the 611 referrals cited above only forty-nine went on to become full investigations, with no protection orders being applied for.

Staff training

There appears to be a level of anxiety amongst social work staff that they are ill-equipped to deal with adults at risk. It appears that changing or formalising the terminology has led to social workers becoming concerned about their skills in this area. Training is an ongoing issue for APCs, particularly rolling this out across staff and organisations, such as health, housing, police and social work. Training of staff has evolved at a local level, although each local authority appears to be approaching this in a staged way, targeting specific groups of staff often in multi-disciplinary groups. Perth and Kinross, for example, have provided multi-disciplinary training as part of a learning and development service training and strategy plan, which also includes working with the public and elected members, with a proposal to develop a specific DVD for the public (Perth and Kinross Adult Protection Committee, 2010).

Future challenges

As the parameters and boundaries of the use of the legislation continue to evolve and develop it appears likely that the ASP will be used in more imaginative ways across a broader range of service user groups. This may include those who abuse alcohol and drugs and work with people who self-harm, although this is a controversial area. In addition, it is expected that referrals are likely to be more focused than at present as experience develops and awareness-raising and training become more systematic.

A further challenge will be the existing financial situation, which may impact on the availability of staff to pursue the development of adult protection at the existing level. For agencies outwith the local authority (which have a statutory responsibility) competing demands to implement new policy agendas with fewer resources may compromise the focus on adult protection when it is no longer the 'flavour of the month'.

Finally, the emergence and implementation of the self-directed support, personalisation agenda is likely to mean that many at risk adults are working with their own personal assistants rather than organisations and holding their own budgets. There is concern that the potential for these adults to have their vulnerabilities exploited may increase with the roll out of this personalisation. Ferguson (2007), for example, argues that the personalisation agenda is about the transfer of risk from the state to the individual, putting them further at risk and increasing powerlessness rather than promoting control. He further suggests that there may be a similar impact on professionals. It has been argued in more recent research on personalisation and risk that personalisation of support can promote effective safeguarding of adults, particularly as it enables and empowers individuals to speak out for themselves (Simpson, 2010). However, this positive approach to personalisation, risk and adult protection requires consistent application of an empowerment model to be realised. Clear support and guidance are, therefore, required for this to happen and indeed this issue features significantly in the biennial reports produced by the APCs for the Scottish Government in 2010.

Potential gaps in legislation

Now that the ASP has been operational for more than three years it is helpful to consider if there are any gaps in the current legislation and what this may mean in practice or for any review of the legislation. The following details some of the key areas practitioners feel need consideration in the future:

- The duty to co-operate/share information should be extended to GPs as it is often difficult to gain compliance when seeking information or for encouraging them to report harm.
- There is no independent body with powers to monitor the use or implementation of the Act – like, for example, the Mental Welfare Commission does for the MHCTSA or the Office of the Public Guardian does for adults with incapacity. In addition, there is no independent overview nationally that has any kind of redress for adults compared to other laws.
- There remains disagreement over whether or not the legislation has 'teeth' and there is also concern over the perceived

limitations of the protection orders. Where an individual breaches a banning order, for example, without power of arrest there is no sanction. Also, how do you 'police' a banning order? There are similarities here to supporting and protecting those who experience domestic violence.

- The links to the criminal justice system continue to be challenging. It is also not clear that removing people will be helpful to the family as a whole: 'Not sure whether you can draw a straight line between what's happened in the past and what we've ended up with.' In addition, if barring orders are used with the main breadwinner in a family, how are the family supposed to live?

Citizenship and early implementation

If we consider the balance of rights and responsibilities to be at the core of competing concepts of citizenship and the conditions attached to achieving full citizenship (Lawson, 2001), it is interesting to note how these competing agendas are emerging in the implementation of the ASP. The balancing of the responsibilities of the state to protect, and through the ASP the responsibilities of local authorities and their partners to enact this protection, and the rights of citizens has been at the centre of the implementation of the ASP. Many of the challenges cited above appear to be linked to a desire to ensure that the state's reach into the protection of adults does not compromise their rights as citizens. Consideration of what constitutes adult protection, for example, and indeed the conceptualisation of what this might look like in practice, appear to be an evolving and contested concept. The key considerations around the evolution of this concept seem to be ensuring human rights and that thresholds are considered within the context of upholding these rights. This is perhaps to be expected because this legislation, as with all protective measures in Scotland (the AWIA and the MHCTSA), is underpinned with principles ensuring that the rights of individuals are safeguarded. Perhaps one of the reasons for the lack of engagement of specific disciplines, particularly health, may be attributed to the protection of citizenship rights, although this can merely be speculation at this stage of implementation and requires a more detailed case analysis.

However, as Lister (1998) argues and as discussed in detail in Chapter 4, being a citizen and acting as a citizen may be the delineating factor between intervention and non-intervention within the ASP framework. What is clear from the above discussion of the conceptualisation of adult protection is that ensuring the rights of individuals are maintained appears to be highly influential in the day-to-day practice within the Scottish legislative context.

There still remains the issue of Section 35 of the Act and the ability to override the consent of an adult who has capacity. As previously discussed, this allows for the lack of consent of the adult to be overridden where there is concern that they have been subjected to undue pressure to withhold their consent. From the limited available statistical information, and considering the variation in how data are collected, it is difficult to be accurate about the use of the undue pressure as a reason for overriding concent. However, the informal data collection discussed by DeSouza (2011) appears to indicate a very low level of application of this aspect of the Act. As with application for other protective orders within the ASP, priority appears to have been given to voluntary measures rather than compelling an individual to conform to protection without their consent. In addition, the fact that the most often used measure is a banning or temporary banning order indicates that the focus of intervention is on the perpetrator rather than the individual experiencing harm.

Conclusion

It is interesting to note that Hogg *et al.* (2009b) consider that even with the introduction of the ASP there are likely to be continuing challenges to the operation of any system to protect adults at risk of harm. In particular, the likelihood of basic operational errors continuing was felt to be high, as were the conceptualisation of what constitutes adult protection and the impact of professional and cultural issues impacting on practice. Perhaps, further consideration also needs to be given to upstream legislation/processes to prevent harm reaching damaging proportions, ensuring that anticipatory and preventative work can be carried out effectively. The ASP may achieve this aim; the outcome of the Scottish Government sponsored evaluation should provide evidence of whether or not this has been achieved.

There appear to be ongoing challenges with regard to the construction of just what constitutes the need for adult protection and of what an adult protection referral should be based on as well as the levels of engagement across the key agencies with particular concerns expressed about health's involvement.

Despite the above, it is clear that adults at risk of harm who may previously have been hidden from view without a route for agencies to 'get their foot in the door' are being able to be engaged. Furthermore, early evidence suggests that, in the majority of cases, protective interventions are being provided on a voluntary basis rather than having to resort to compulsory measures. Therefore, whilst it is still likely that those outwith generally accepted paradigms of citizenship are more likely to be subject to the protection orders within the ASP, it appears as though practice is evolving to ensure their rights are protected, with a focus on short-term orders and voluntary engagement with services. This means that there is equal consideration being given to support and protection – a clear goal of those involved in developing this legislation.

CHAPTER 6

The Way Forward

This book has considered the evolution and implementation of adult protection in the UK through the lens of citizenship. This chapter will bring together the key themes that emerge throughout the book and will consider the impact of these on the future of this agenda, drawing on early experience of the implementation of the ASP in Scotland.

What has become evident is that interventions into the lives of adults to provide support and protection are both complex and ethically challenging to undertake. It is evident that, in Scotland, considerable emphasis is being put upon the upholding of individuals' rights in the way in which practice is developing. In addition, supportive approaches to preventing harm continuing appear to take priority in practice, further protecting the rights of adults who may require assistance. This focus on supportive, voluntary measures, which include the adult in the process, reflects both the personalisation agenda and an outcomes-led approach to assessment. However, there are still key issues for consideration in the future development of the legislation and further work to be undertaken to assess the extent to which the ASP and other adult protection measures are meeting their key aims and objectives in an appropriate manner.

The concepts of abuse and vulnerability have underpinned much of the development of adult protection procedures throughout the UK, and there appears to be considerable consensus in legislative terms over what constitutes abuse and/or harm. These definitions are clearly socially constructed and are subject to interpretations, which may be fluid over time, depending upon the prevailing social mores. Therefore, future development within adult protection will require flexibility to absorb and reflect these cultural changes. Perceptions of what constitute abuse and/or harm also need to be continually challenged and updated to ensure equality for those considered at risk (Penhale and Parker, 2008). Examples of harm perpetrated against adults discussed in Chapter 1 clearly indicate how the changes in what is appropriate behaviour have altered significantly over the last twenty years. The main focus of these changes has been on empowering adults, particularly those with disabilities, to support and protect themselves and enabling appropriate risk taking. In addition, the increase in both support for and recognition of the rights of those deemed 'at risk' or vulnerable has been cemented through the European Human Rights legislation as well as the recent convention on the rights of persons with disabilities (UN, 2006). Terminology has been shown to be important as inappropriate labelling can situate the vulnerability to harm and/or abuse within the adult themselves rather than within their broader context, thus further isolating and discriminating against the adult.

Given the evolutionary shifts in the social construction of the core concepts that underpin adult protection, it is clear that there has to be flexibility to accommodate these changes in understanding and challenging social norms. *Supporting Vulnerable Adults* has, therefore, considered three key areas – choice, citizenship and capacity – within the lives of adults and how these concepts have impacted on the adult protection action in the UK, and how these can reinforce or interact with each other.

Choice

As has been discussed earlier, an adult's right to self-determination, to make choices about how he or she lives their life, has, it could be argued, been challenged by the introduction of aspects of the ASP in Scotland (Stewart, 2011). In particular, Section 35, the ability to override consent to intervention where undue pressure can be evidenced, under the ASP has proven controversial both throughout the passage of the Act and in early implementation. The main focus of this controversy has been the extent of the reach of the state in undermining individual decision-making for adults who have capacity to make their own life choices. It is notable that this requirement does not rely on a lack of capacity or incapacity being confirmed but on concerns over undue pressure being exerted on the adult to withhold their consent to intervention under the legislation. Despite this legislative route to remove the right of adults to choose how to live their lives, Patrick and Smith (2009) indicate that to do so may constitute a breach of the adults' human rights. To date, no test of this under the ASP has been explored in practice.

By removing an element of choice for adults and by pursuing a structured adult protection framework, it could be argued that the UK – and more broadly and specifically in this case Scotland – has adopted a paternalistic approach to providing support and protection for its citizens. This concept suggests that the interference of the state of an individual with another person, against their will, and defended or motivated by a claim that the person interfered with will be better off or protected from harm is paternalistic (Thaler and Sunstein, 2003). Indeed, many proponents of a libertarian approach to paternalism (e.g. Thaler and Sunstein, 2003) view it as inevitable and desirable that public institutions will influence behaviour, while also respecting freedom of choice. They argue that this is particularly the case and indeed unavoidable where opinions and decisions are ill-formed or influenced by external forces, as could be illustrated within many examples of adults at risk of harm. However, labelling actions or, in this case, policy as paternalistic can be seen as derogatory or to be implicitly critical. Paternalism may, however, be more appropriate or justifiable in adult protection where it could be argued, for example, that more harm than good can be evidenced or that any reduction in autonomy in the short term may increase autonomy in the longer term.

It would clearly be difficult to argue that adult protection was a negative development in the range of supports available within adult care. Indeed, there can be little debate that, in some cases, intervention is required to provide support and protection to adults who have the capacity to make their own choices to prevent harm, particularly given the number of high-profile cases, some of which were discussed in Chapter 2. Therefore, perhaps we should re-examine how concepts of paternalism aid our understanding of the impact of adult protection on citizens of the UK.

Proponents of soft-paternalism contend that time-conditional interference by the state is acceptable only when it is necessary to determine whether the person being interfered with is acting voluntarily and knowledgably (DeMarneffe, 2006). To relate this directly to adult protection, particularly where consent can be overridden, the argument would be that the person must possess full knowledge and awareness of the impact of decision-making, which would lead to harm. However, if the adult did have full knowledge and insight, with no external pressure being brought to bear to view things in a particular way, then he or she must be allowed to make their own choice about proceeding with any determined course of action. This can be further considered with the framework of bounded rationality, which suggests that human beings can make rational decisions only when they have the appropriate information available to them (Gigerenzer and Selten, 2002). In adult protection terms, therefore, it is apparent that the element of support is crucial in ensuring information is made available so that rational decisions are taken and adults empowered to take control of their own lives.

It could be argued that the ASP and the broader adult protection agenda in the UK are largely a product of soft-paternalism, with only those aspects undertaken without the consent of the adult being considered paternalistic in nature. In addition, the focus on support as well as protection aids in empowering adults and enabling them to secure their rights for themselves suggest that long-term outcomes for adults are more likely to be positive following intervention.

Citizenship

Consideration of the impact of adult support and protection procedures in Scotland and elsewhere in the UK on the citizenship rights of adults has been discussed throughout this book. It has become evident that there is a potential model of citizenship, being a citizen, rather than acting as a citizen (Lister, 1998), which may make citizenship more fragile for this particular group of adults as well as statutory intervention more likely. Consequently, as political landscapes and ideologies have changed, a model of citizenship that relies upon responsibilities as much as rights (MacKay, 2011) has evolved.

Supporting Vulnerable Adults has argued that those adults whose citizenship has been compromised, or made fragile by virtue of age, poverty, disability or other vulnerabilities, are more likely to be subject to adult protection procedures than those who have not. Essentially, those adults who are citizens but not acting as citizens are more vulnerable to having intervention imposed in their life with or without their consent. By attaching conditions to citizenship we immediately exclude sections of society who are unable to meet those conditions and compromise their ability to claim their rights and, ironically, to meet their responsibilities. We need to consider, therefore, whether or not these conditions are appropriate for all or whether they require adaptation to include the broadest range of citizens and so enable them to make appropriate contributions and to further protect their rights.

For those working within adult protection frameworks, the impact of citizenship made fragile by an ascribed vulnerability needs to be considered in all interactions and assessments of individuals. This should include the safeguarding of adults' rights as central to any process to implement adult protection. Within the Scottish context, protecting the rights of adults is central to the legislation and guidance; however, it could argued that the power to override the consent of the adult compromises the rights-based approach to a certain extent and further erodes the citizenship rights of the adult.

Early evidence of empowerment and voluntary engagement being the approach taken to the implementation of the ASP in Scotland clearly suggests that practice is promoting an equal focus on support and protection. Indeed, one of the main arguments for not legislating on adult protection in other jurisdictions of the UK is that the same outcomes can be achieved from policy and guidance if only it were used as intended and that to develop legislation would not solve this particular challenge.

By ensuring this balance between support and protection, it could be argued that any inequity in citizenship rights can be somewhat ameliorated; as Harris (1999) notes, some adults require support to claim their citizenship rights. Indeed, promoting the support element of the ASP could lead to enhanced citizenship in the longer term by enabling empowerment through support and enabling the adult to retain control of their own lives rather than being a passive recipient of support and protection. In addition, as Beckett (2006) argues, if we can accept the notion of universal vulnerability – that we could all be made vulnerable by the context in which we live – then we avoid marking out these groups and ensure equality of citizenship rights.

Capacity

Providing support and protection to those who lack capacity in Scotland falls within the parameters of the Adults with Incapacity (Scotland) Act 2000, while the issue of capacity and the ASP has been much considered within this book – in particular with regard to whether or not the legislation should and/or can provide care and support to those who lack capacity. Across other jurisdictions in the UK substitute decision-making for those who lack capacity also largely remains outside the parameters of adult protection procedures (e.g. Mental Capacity Act; see DH, 2005). Therefore, having capacity to make decisions about your own life is more often than not the difference between having state-sponsored intrusion in your life or not. In essence, those who lack capacity give the responsibility of claiming their citizenship rights to others to claim on their behalf. Those who have capacity but are still subject to state-sponsored intervention under Section 35 of the ASP, it could be argued, have compromised capacity due to external influences or context: for example, where they are in fear for their well-being if they do not provide money to a relative. Alternatively, in the example given above, they may have reached the bounds of their rationality, which has been limited due to external factors influencing their decision-making process.

Consideration of capacity and adult protection is further confused because that there appears to be disagreement over whether or not the ASP was developed for those who lack capacity. This ambiguity may be related to the specific role of this legislation with its focus on support and protection. It is difficult to assert that the triage model emerging in practice was intentional, but as it stands this model appears to enable those who previously were hidden from services, including those who lack capacity, to be supported and protected via the appropriate legislation and/or, in the main, through voluntarily engaging with services. Therefore, it could asserted that only those adults whose capacity or rationality has been compromised by external factors are likely to be subject to the aspects of adult protection which override the consent of the adult. Those to whom support can be provided to alter the context or situation that has affected their capacity are more likely to benefit from voluntary engagement within the broader voluntary aspects of adult protection.

Conclusion

There were and, rightly, continue to be concerns about the parameters of statutory intervention in the lives of adults. However, the research underpinning this book highlights that, without a formal legislative process, adults at risk of harm may remain unsupported and unprotected in their communities and so experience continuing harm. As highlighted in Chapter 5, for practitioners in the early implementation of the ASP, the mere prospect of compulsion has, in their view, led to an increase in voluntary engagement with adults at risk of harm and their families.

Therefore, exploration of appropriate processes and consideration of the parameters of these processes are essential to ensure that the rights of adults are protected. The recent review of the *No Secrets* guidance (DH, 2009) highlighted that 68% of respondents felt legislation should be introduced in England because of the need to balance choice and safeguards. This balance appears to be effectively undertaken in practice using a combination of practice wisdom and clear guidance for practitioners and their agencies. In Scotland, for example, codes of practice and guidance alongside practice experience appear to be evolving to counteract and ameliorate concerns about the overreach of the state into the lives of adults to ensure, perhaps, that soft-paternalistic approaches outweigh hard-paternalism in the majority of cases. In addition, the small number of protection orders being considered and applied for under the ASP legislation suggest that these are appropriately considered as a last resort in line with the principles that underpin the triangle of protection in Scotland. For the small number of adults who require to be compelled to allow intervention within an adult protection framework, there is an argument to suggest that these are adults whose capacity to make decisions for themselves has been compromised by external factors, thereby limiting their rational decision-making: for example, whether or not to remain in harmful situations.

A number of key themes have emerged throughout the reviews of the various adult protection policies across the UK. For future development of policy the main areas for consideration appear to include: consideration of the language used to ensure it does not disempower or stigmatise adults; any policy developments should promote empowerment for adults to support themselves and not be passive in their own lives; consideration of possible sanctions with regard to non-compliance (e.g. the banning orders with powers of arrest within the ASP, which focus on the perpetrator of the harm and not the subject); and, finally, the possibility of compelling key stakeholders to work within the guidance by creating a legal duty.

In addition to the above, there is no question that links with criminal justice systems over acts of criminality such as theft and various types of assault are also crucial in ensuring harm is prevented on a continuous basis. This further promotes a message of zero tolerance about harm being perpetrated against adults whose ability to protect themselves has been compromised by their context in whatever form. Perhaps, more fundamentally, the work of adult protection professionals from whatever background would be greatly enhanced with increased clarity over the nature of the population likely to experience this form of harm and/or abuse. Significant work, for example, is required to explore prevalence rates and the harm experienced by people with learning disabilities, mental health problems and physical disabilities.

Whilst there remains a clear element of wait and see about the impact of the implementation of the ASP in Scotland, there is some limited evidence to suggest that it is providing support and protection to a group of service users who may previously have remained hidden, through voluntary engagement. It is to be hoped that the voluntary nature of this engagement will produce greater levels of autonomy and independence for adults in the longer term. Detailed analysis of case examples from across the UK is required to consider the extent to which the citizenship rights of those individuals have been compromised or curtailed through their involvement in adult protection frameworks and, indeed, to examine key factors in securing successful outcomes.

More broadly, the future of adult protection remains unclear across much of the UK. There is a clear divergence between approaches roughly split between a public-protection and rights-based approach (MacKay, 2011). So far, England and Wales (e.g. DH, 2009) have rejected the notion of a need for additional consolidating legislation to protect adults at risk of harm, preferring to emphasise appropriate use of existing measures, despite clear failures in the past. What is apparent is that adult protection is evolving at a rapid pace, with detailed consideration being given to all of the areas discussed within this book. What is currently lacking is clear evidence of the impact both policy and legislative process are having on outcomes for adults. Once a clear baseline is established, comparisons between the jurisdictional approaches should aid in developing adult protection procedures, which support and protect within a framework that promotes adults claiming their citizenship rights and being empowered to protect themselves from harm in the longer term, even if this requires ongoing support.

REFERENCES

Table of Statutes

Aberdeenshire Adult Protection Committee (2010) *Biennial Report 2008–2010*, Aberdeen: Aberdeenshire Adult Protection Committee. URL: www.aberdeenshire.gov.uk/about/departments/FinalAPCBiennialReport2008–2010.pdf (accessed June 2011)

Action on Elder Abuse (2007) *Briefing Paper: The UK Study of Abuse and Neglect of Older People*, London: Action on Elder Abuse. URL: www.globalaging.org/elderrights/world/2007/Briefing_paper_Prevalence.pdf (accessed June 2011)

ADSS (2005) *Safeguarding Adults: A National Framework of Standards for Good Practice and Outcomes in Adult Protection Work*, Association of Directors of Social Services: London

Adult Protection Renfrewshire (2010) *Renfrewshire Adult Protection Committee Biennial Report September 2010*, Paisley: Renfrewshire Adult Protection Committee. URL: www.renfrewshire.gov.uk/ilwwcm/publishing.nsf/AttachmentsByTitle/sw-RAPCBiReport.pdf/$FILE/sw-RAPCBiReport.pdf (accessed June 2011)

Argyll and Bute Adult Protection Committee (2010) *1st Biennial Report April 2008–March 2010*, Oban: Argyll and Bute Adult Protection Committee. URL: www.scotland.gov.uk/Resource/Doc/924/0119639.pdf (accessed June 2011)

Atkinson, J. M. (2006) *Public and Private Protection: Civil Mental Health Legislation*, Edinburgh: Dunedin Academic Press: Edinburgh

Baker, A. (1975) 'Granny bashing', *Modern Geriatrics,* Vol. 5, No. 8, pp. 20–4

Barnes, M. and Bowl, R. (2001) *Taking Over the Asylum: Empowerment and Mental Health*, Houndsmill: Palgrave Macmillan

BBC (2007a) 'Three jailed over shed prisoner'. Available at URL: http://news.bbc.co.uk/1/hi/england/gloucestershire/6284184.stm (accessed 13 February 2011)

BBC (2007b) 'Hillside murderers get life terms'. Available at URL: http://news.bbc.co.uk/1/hi/wales/south_east/6624515.stm (accessed 13 January 2011)

BBC (2008) 'Review of vulnerable adult care'. Available at URL: http://news.bbc.co.uk/1/hi/uk/7672972.stm (accessed 13 February 2011)

Beckett, A. (2006) *Citizenship and Vulnerability: Disability and Issues of Social and Political Engagement*, Houndsmill: Palgrave Macmillan

Bennett, G., Kingston, P. and Penhale, B. (1997) *The Dimensions of Elder Abuse: Perspectives for the Practitioner*. Basingstoke: Macmillan

Blair, T. (1996) *New Britain: My Vision of a Young Country*, London: Fourth Estate

Bornat, J. and Blytheway, B. (2010) 'Perceptions and presentations of living with everyday risk in later life', *British Journal of Social Work*, Vol. 40, No. 4, pp. 1118–34

Boyle A, Himsworth C, Loux A and MacQueen H (Eds)(2002) *Human Rights and Scots Law*. Hart: OXford

Brown, H. (2003) 'What is financial abuse', *The Journal of Adult Protection*, Vol. 5, No. 2, pp. 3–10

Burston, G. (1977) 'Do your elderly patients lie in fear of being battered?', *Modern Geriatrics*, Vol. 7, No. 20, pp. 54–5

Calder, B. (2010) *A guide to the Adult Support and Protection (Scotland) Act 2007*, Dundee: Dundee University Press

Cardono, O. D. (1999) 'Environmental management and disaster prevention: Holistic risk assessment and management', in Ingleton, J. (ed.) *Natural Disaster Management*, London: Tudor Rose

Cogan, J. J. and Derricott, R. (2000) *Citizenship for the Twenty-First Century: An International Perspective on Education*, London: Routledge

Commission for Healthcare Audit and Inspection (2006) *Joint Investigation into the Provision of Services for People with Learning Disabilities at Cornwall Partnership NHS Trust*, London: Commission for Healthcare Audit and Inspection. URL: www.cqc.org.uk/_db/_documents/cornwall_investigation_report.pdf (accessed March 2011)

Community Care Magazine (2009), *Consultation on No Secrets Guidance*, 26 November, p. 8

Cooper, C., Selwood, A. and Livingston, G. (2008), 'The prevalence of elder abuse and neglect: A systematic review', *Age and Ageing*, Vol. 37, No. 2, pp. 151–60

DeMarneffe, P. (2006) 'Avoiding paternalism', *Philosophy and Public Affairs*, Vol. 34, pp. 64–94

Demos (2004), *Personalisation Through Participation*, London: Demos

DeSouza, V. (2011) 'The Adult Support and Protection Act (Scotland) 2007 – initial impact and emerging themes', *Action on Elder Abuse Action Points*, Vol. 43 (January/February)

DH (1993) *No Longer Afraid: The Safeguarding of Older People in Domestic Settings.* London: HMSO

DH (2000) *No Secrets Guidance,* London: HMSO

DH (2009) *Safeguarding Adults – Report on the Consultation on the Review of No Secrets; Guidance on Developing and Implementing Multi-Agency Policies and Procedures to Protect Vulnerable Adults from Abuse,* London: Department of Health. Available from URL: www.dh.gov.uk/en/Consultations/Reponse-stoconsultations/DH_102764 (accessed 11 July 2011)

DHSSPS (2007) *The Bamford Review of Mental Health and Learning Disability (Northern Ireland) A Comprehensive Legislative Framework: Executive Summary,* Belfast: DHSSPS. URL: www.dhsspsni.gov.uk/legal-issues-exec-utive-summary.pdf (accessed July 2011)

DHSSPS (2009) *Reforming Northern Ireland's Adult Protection Infrastructure,* Belfast: DHSSPS

Dwyer, P. (2004) *Understanding Social Citizenship: Themes and Perspectives for Policy and Practice,* Bristol: The Policy Press

Eastman, M. and Sutton, M. (1982) 'Granny battering', *Geriatric Medicine,* Vol. 12], No. 11 (November) pp. 11–15

Faulks, K. (2000) *Citizenship,* London: Routledge

Ferguson I. (2007) 'Increasing user choice or privatising risk? The antinomies of personalisation', *British Journal of Social Work,* Vol. 37, No. 3, pp. 381–403

Fife Adult Protection Committee (2010) *Biennial Report 2008–2010,* Glenrothes: Fife Adult Protection Committee. URL: http://www.scotland.gov.uk/Resource/Doc/924/0119731.pdf (accessed March 2011)

Gigerenzer, G. and Selten, R. (2002) *Bounded Rationality,* Cambridge: MIT Press

Glasby, J. (2003) 'Bringing down the 'Berlin Wall': The health and social care divide', *British Journal of Social Work,* Vol. 33, No. 7, pp. 969–75

Harris, J. (1999) 'State social work and social citizenship in Britain: From clientism to consumerism', *British Journal of Social Work,* Vol. 29, No. 6, pp. 915–37

Hewitt, D. (2009) 'Not just in the Mental Capacity Act: Using the law to protect vulnerable adults', *Journal of Adult Protection,* Vol. 11, No. 2 (May), pp. 25–31

Hogg, J., Johnson, F., Daniel, B. and Ferguson, A. (2009a) *Interagency Collaboration in Adult Support and Protection in Scotland: Processes and Barriers. Vol. 1: Final Report,* Dundee: White Top Research Unit, University of Dundee

Hogg, J., Johnson, F., Daniel, B. and Ferguson, A. (2009b) *Interagency Collaboration in Adult Support and Protection in Scotland: Processes and Barriers. Vol. 2: Recommendations,* Dundee, White Top Research Unit, University of Dundee

House of Commons (2004) *Select Committee on Health Second Report,* London: HMSO. Available from URL: www.publications.parliament.uk/pa/cm200304/cmselect/cmhealth/111/11103.htm (accessed 11 July 2011)

Hussein, S., Manthorpe, J. and Penhale, B. (2007) 'Public perceptions of the neglect and mistreatment of older people: Findings from a UK survey', *Ageing and Society,* Vol. 27, No. 6, pp. 919–40

Keenan, T. (2011) 'Crossing the Acts' The Support and Protection of Adults at risk with Mental Disorder Across the Scottish Legislative Frameworks,

Venture: Birmingham

Kymlicka, W. (1995) 'Multi-cultural citizenship', in Shaft, G. (ed.) *The Citizenship Debate: A Reader*, London: University of Minnesota Press

Law Commission (1995) *Mental Incapacity*, Consultation Paper No. 231, London: HMSO

Lawson, H. (2001) 'Active citizenship in schools and the community', *Curriculum Journal*, Vol. 12, No. 2, pp. 163–78

Leslie, S. and Pritchard, J. (2009) 'A review of relevant legislation in adult protection', in Pritchard, J. (ed.) (2009) *Good Practice in the Law and Safeguarding Adults: Criminal Justice and Adult Protection*, London: Kingsley

Lister, R. (1997) *Citizenship: Feminist Perspectives*, Basingstoke: Macmillan

Lister R (1998) 'In from the margins: Citizenship, inclusion and exclusion', in Barry, H. C. (ed.), *Social Exclusion and Social Work: Issues of Theory, Policy and Practice*, Lyme Regis: Russell House Publishing

Lynch, T. (1992) *Education for citizenship in a multi-cultural society*, London: Cassell

McCreadie, C. (1996) *Elder Abuse: An Update On Research*, London: HMSO

MacKay, K. (2008) 'The Scottish adult support and protection legal framework', *Journal of Adult Protection*, Vol. 10, No. 4, pp. 25–36

MacKay, K. (2009) 'The Scottish legal context of adult support and protection', in Pritchard, J. (ed.) (2009) *Good Practice in the Law and Safeguarding Adults: Criminal Justice and Adult Protection,* London: Jessica Kingsley

MacKay, K. (2011) 'Compounding conditional citizenship: To what extent does Scottish and English mental health law increase or diminish citizenship?', *British Journal of Social Work*. Available from URL: http://bjsw.oxfordjournals.org/content/early/2011/05/18/bjsw.bcr010.abstract (accessed 11 July 2011)

McLauchlin. K. (2008) *Social Work, Politics and Society*, Bristol: Policy Press

Magill J, Yeates V. and Longley M. (2010) Review of In Safe Hands: A Review of the Welsh Assembly Government's Guidance on the Protection of Vulnerable Adults in Wales. Welsh Institute of Health and Social Care, University of Glamorgan.

Mandelstam M. (2009) *Safeguarding Vulnerable Adults and the Law*, London: Jessica Kingsley

Mantell, A. and Scragg, T. (2008) *Safeguarding Adults in Social Work*, Exeter: Learning Matters

Marshall, T. (1950) 'Citizenship and social class', in Pierson, C. and Castles, F. G. (eds) (2000) *The Welfare Reader*, Cambridge: Polity Press

Mooney, G. and Scott, G. (eds.) (2005), *Exploring Social Policy in the 'New' Scotland*, Bristol: Policy Press

Nair, P. and Mayberry, J. (1995) 'The compulsory removal of elderly people in England and Wales under Section 47 of the National Assistance Act and its 195 amendment: A survey of its implementation in England and Wales in 1998 and 1989', *Age and Ageing*, Vol. 24, No. 3, pp. 180–4

National Assembly for Wales (2000) *In Safe Hands. Implementing Adult Protection in Wales*, Cardiff: National Assembly for Wales

North Lanarkshire Adult Protection Committee (2010) *Biennial Report,*

Motherwell: North Lanarkshire Adult Protection Committee. URL: www.northlanarkshire.gov.uk/CHttpHandler.ashx?id=5813&p=0 (accessed June 2011)

Northern Ireland Social Services Board (2006) *Safeguarding Vulnerable Adults: Regional Adult Protection Policy and Procedural Guidance,* Ballymena: Social Services Directorate

Northern Ireland Assembly (2008) *Reform of the Mental Health Legislation in the UK,* Research paper 41/09, Belfast: Northern Ireland Assembly

Ogg, J. and Bennett, G. (1992) 'Elder abuse in Britain', *British Medical Journal,* Vol. 305, pp. 998–9. Available from URL: www.bmj.com/content/317/7169/1389.2.full (accessed 11 July 2011)

O'Keefe, M., Hills, A., Doyle, M., McCreadie, C. *et al.* (2007) *UK Study of Abuse and Neglect of Older People,* London: Department of Health

Paine, T. (1995) *Rights of Man, Common Sense and Other Political Writings,* Oxford: Oxford University Press

Patrick, H. and Smith, N. (2009) *Adult Protection and the Law in Scotland,* Haywards Heath, West Sussex: Bloomsbury Professional

Penhale, B. (1993) 'The abuse of elderly people: Considerations for practice', *British Journal of Social Work,* Vol. 23, No. 2, pp. 95–112

Penhale, B. and Parker, J. (2008) *Working with Vulnerable Adults,* Abingdon: Routledge

Penhale, B. and Parker, J. with Kingston, P. (2000) *Elder Abuse,* Birmingham: Venture Press

Penhale, B., Perkins, N., Pinkney, L., Reid, D., Hussein, S. and Manthorpe, J. (2007) 'Partnership and regulation' in *Adult Protection: The Effectiveness of Multi-Agency Working and the Regulatory Framework in Adult Protection,* Sheffield: University of Sheffield. Available from URL: www.prap.group.shef.ac.uk (accessed 11 July 2011)

Perth and Kinross Adult Protection Committee (2010) *Perth and Kinross Adult Protection Committee Biennial Report 2008–2010,* Perth: Perth and Kinross Adult Protection Committee. URL: www.pkc.gov.uk/NR/rdonlyres/0DAC247C-D96E-45F9-A378-457793ED6815/0/PKASAPCommitteeBiennialReport20082010.pdf (accessed June 2011)

Phillipson, C. and Biggs, S. (1995) 'Elder abuse: A critical overview', in Kingston, P. and Penhale, B. *Family Violence and the Caring Professions,* Basingstoke: Macmillan

Pilgrim, D. (2007) 'New "mental health" legislation for England and Wales: Some aspects of consensus and conflict', *Journal of Social Policy,* Vol. 36, No. 1, pp. 79–95

Pritchard J. (Ed) (2009) *Good Practice in the Law and Safegurading Adults: Criminal Justice and Adult Protection,* London: Jessica Kingsley

Rawls, J. (1998) 'Justice as fairness in the liberal polity', in Shafir, G. (ed.), *The Citizenship Debates. A Reader,* London: University of Minnesota Press

Regional Adult Protection Forum (2009) *Protocol for Joint Investigation of Alleged and Suspected Cases of Abuse of Vulnerable Adults,* Belfast: Regional Adult Protection Forum. Available from URL: www.hscboard.hscni.net/consult/Policies/Protocol%20for%20Joint%20Investigation%20of%20

Alleged%20and%20Suspected%20Cases%20of%20Abuse%20of%20Vulnerable%20Adults%20-%20July%202009.pdf (accessed 20 September 2011)

Robb, B. (1967) *Sans Everything: A Case to Answer*, London: Nelson

Robson, C. (2002) *Real World Research: A Resource for Social Scientists and Practitioner Researchers*, Oxford: Blackwell

Scottish Executive (2001) *Vulnerable Adults: Consultation Paper*, Edinburgh: Blackwell. Available from URL: www.scotland.gov.uk/Publications/2001/12/10399/File-1 (accessed 11 July 2011)

Scottish Executive (2004a) *Home At Last? The National Implementation Group Report of the Short Life Working Group on Hospital Closure and Service Reprovision*, Edinburgh: Blackwell. Available from URL: www.scotland.gov.uk/Publications/2004/01/18741/31584 (accessed 11 July 2011)

Scottish Executive (2004b) *Investigations into Scottish Borders Council and NHS Borders Services for People with Learning Disabilities: Joint Statement from the Mental Welfare Commission and the Social Work Services Inspectorate*. Available from URL: www.scotland.gov.uk/Publications/2004/05/19333/36719 (accessed 11 July 2011)

Scottish Executive (2005) *Review of Literature Relating to Mental Health Legislation*. Edinburgh: Blackwell. Available from URL: www.scotland.gov.uk/Publications/2005/07/1595204/52064 (accessed 11 July 2011)

Scottish Executive (2007) *A Review of Literature on Effective Interventions That Prevent and Respond to Harm Against Adults*. Edinburgh: Blackwell. Available from URL: www.scotland.gov.uk/Resource/Doc/203554/0054266.pdf (accessed 11 July 2011)

Scottish Government (2009) Adult Support and Protection (Scotland) Act (2007) Code of Practice 2009/01/30112831, Blackwell: Edinburgh

Scottish Government (2010) *Act Against Harm: Adult Support and Protection Lead Officer Event*. Edinburgh: Scottish Government. Available from URL: www.scotland.gov.uk/Resource/Doc.924/0111379.doc (accessed 11 July 2101)

Scottish Government (2011) *Self-Directed Support: A National Strategy for Scotland*. Edinburgh: Blackwell. Available from URL: www.scotland.gov.uk/Publications/2010/02/05133942/0 (accessed 11 July 2011)

Scottish Law Commission (1997) *Report on Vulnerable Adults*, Scottish Law Commission No. 158, Edinburgh: The Stationery Office

Simpson, B. (2010) *Practical Approaches to Safeguarding and Personalisation*, London: Department of Health

Smith, N. and Patrick, H. (2009) *Adult Protection and the Law*, Edinburgh: Bloomsbury Professional

South Lanarkshire Council (2010) *South Lanarkshire Adult Protection Committee Biennial Report October 2010*, Hamilton: South Lanarkshire Adult Protection Committee. URL: www.southlanarkshire.gov.uk/download/4555/adult_protection_committee_biennial_report_2010 (accessed September 2011)

Stewart, A. (2008) *Common Themes in Inquiries and Investigations Undertaken by the Mental Welfare Commission for Scotland between 1998 and 2007*, Edinburgh: Mental Welfare Commission for Scotland

Stewart, A. (2011) 'Adult protection in the UK: Key issues for early career social workers', in Taylor, R., Hill, M. and McNeil, F. (eds) (2001) *Early Professional Development for Social Workers*, Birmingham: Venture

Thaler, R. H. and Sunstein, C. R. (2003) 'Designing better choices', *American Economic Review*, Vol. 93, No. 2, pp. 175–9

Townsend, P. (1962) *The Last Refuge*, London: Routledge

UN (2006) *UN Convention on the Rights of Persons with Disabilities*. Available from URL: www.un.org/disabilities/convention/conventionfull.shtml (accessed 11 July 2011)

Vickers, R. (2004) *Case Review in Respect of MP*, Sheffield: Sheffield Adult Protection Committee

Volunteer Now (2010) *Safeguarding Vulnerable Adults – A Shared Responsibility*, Belfast: Volunteer Now

Webb, S. A. (2006) *Social Work in a Risk Society*, Basingstoke: Palgrave Macmillan

Welsh Institute for Health and Social Care (2010) *Review of 'In Safe Hands; A Review of the Welsh Assembly Government's Guidance on the Protection of Vulnerable Adults in Wales'*, Pontypridd: University of Glamorgan

Western Mail (2009) *Protection of Elderly Just an Illusion*. Available from URL: www.walesonline.co.uk/news/wales-news/2009/06/11/protection-of-elderly-just-an-illusion-91466–23841195 (accessed 11 June 2009)

Young, I. M. (1990) *Justice and the Politics of Difference*, Princeton NJ: Princeton University Press

INDEX